MUSIC HALL

MUSIC HALL

How a City Built a Theater and a Theater Shaped a City

BY J. DENNIS ROBINSON

GREAT LIFE PRESS
Rye, New Hampshire
2019

published for

The Music Hall
28 Chestnut Street, Portsmouth NH 03801
www.themusichall.org

by

Great Life Press
Rye, New Hampshire 03870
www.greatlifepress.com

ISBN: 978-1-938394-34-8
Library of Congress Control Number: 2019913435

BOOK DESIGN: Grace Peirce, J. Dennis Robinson

TITLE PAGE ART CREDIT: Kaitlyn Huwe

JACKET PHOTOS: David J. Murray, ClearEyePhoto.com.
Front: Pop and country singer-songwriter k.d. lang on
the Music Hall stage.
Back: The redesigned Music Hall streetscape in
downtown Portsmouth, New Hampshire

Publisher's Cataloging-in-Publication Data

Names: Robinson, J. Dennis, author.
Title: Music hall : how a city built a theater and a theater shaped a city /
by J. Dennis Robinson.
    Description: Rye, NH: Great Life Press, 2019.
Identifiers: LCCN 2019913435 | ISBN 978-1-938394-34-8
Subjects: LCSH Music Hall (Portsmouth, N.H.) | Performing arts--
New Hampshire--Portsmouth--History--20th century. | Portsmouth (N.H.)--
Buildings, structures, etc. | Portsmouth (N.H.)--History. | Historic buildings--
New Hampshire--Portsmouth. | BISAC HISTORY / United States / State &
Local / New England (CT, MA, ME, NH, RI, VT)
Classification: LCC PN2277.P582 R63 2019 | DDC 791/.09742/6--dc23

Also by J. Dennis Robinson

MYSTERY ON THE ISLES OF SHOALS
Closing the Case on the Smuttynose Ax Murders of 1873

UNDER THE ISLES OF SHOALS
Archaeology & Discovery on Smuttynose Island

AMERICA'S PRIVATEER
Lynx and the War of 1812

STRAWBERY BANKE
A Seacoast Museum 400 Years in the Making

WENTWORTH BY THE SEA
The Life & Times of a Grand Hotel

STRIKING BACK
The Fight to End Child Labor Exploitation

JESSE JAMES
Legendary Rebel and Outlaw

LORD BALTIMORE
Founder of Maryland

RICH WITH CHILDREN
An Italian Family Comes to America
(With Lynne Vachon)

❧

Contents

We would like to acknowledge the people who have led the
Friends of the Music Hall throughout the years

Executive Directors
Mary Kelley (1989–1992)
Donald Tirabassi (1992–1996)
Ann Dumaresq (1996–1997)
Paul Armstrong (1997–1999)
Jeffrey Gable (1999–2003)
Gail VanHoy Carolan—Interim (2003–2004)
Patricia Lynch (2004–2020)

Presidents of the Board of Trustees
David E. Choate, III (1989–1993)
Christine M. Dwyer (1993–1997)
Peter Bowman (1997–2000)
Patricia Gianotti (2000–2002)
Ronald Rakaseder (2002–2003)
Gail VanHoy Carolan (2003–2007)
Michael C. Harvell, Esq. (2007–2011)
David Hills (2011–2013)
Robert W. Hickey, MD (2013–2015)
Barbara Henry (2015–2017)
Jay McSharry (2017–2019)
Edwin Garside (2019–present)

ॐ

Author's Acknowledgments

My deepest appreciation to Patricia Lynch, who proposed this book and then let me loose to tell the story of the theater she has so profoundly influenced, and to Music Hall historian Zhana Morris who was supportive from the first paragraph and illustration to the last. Thanks also to Jameson French, Jessica Griffin, Gail VanHoy Carolan, Monte Bohanan, and other stellar Music Hall supporters and staff. I am indebted, as always, to the staff of the Portsmouth Athenaeum where much of the Music Hall collection is archived.

My team of expert readers, fact checkers, and typo annihilators included Kathryn Cowdrey, Terry Cowdrey, Richard M. Candee, Kathleen Soldati, Ann Beattie, Tricia Peone, Jim Cerny, Genevieve Aichele, Tom Hardiman, Karen Bouffard, Stephanie Seacord, John Mayer, Kelly Cormier, and Linn Schultz.

Among the many people who offered help along the way, my thanks to Malia Ebel at the NH Historical Society and Sabina Beauchard at the Massachusetts Historical Society, Charles Griffin, Gerald M. Zelin, Trevor Bartlett, Robin Albert, Marguerite Matthews, Margaret Talcott, Doug Nelson, Lisa Donnelly, Jeff Warner, Senator Martha Fuller Clark, Chris Dwyer, Randa McNamara, Jeff Warner, Emily Grandstaff, Scott Weintraub, Elaine Finkowski, Rod Watterson, John Tabor, Sandra Rux, Janet Jones, Gerald W.R. Ward, Kevin LaFond, Cheryl Farley, Kim Lingard, and Colleen Michel. And a tip of the hat to fellow history authors Eric Lehman (*Becoming Tom Thumb*) and John Hodgson (*Richard Potter*). It was a pleasure, once again, to work with the talented designer and publisher Grace Peirce and to share the work of the phenomenal photographer, David J. Murray of ClearEyePhoto.com.

And finally, thanks to all my fellow unsung underpaid journalists who reported the ups and downs of the Music Hall over the decades. In a break from style manual convention, the bibliography at the back includes some key newspaper articles used in researching this book with reporter bylines where available. ❧

Introduction

I was scared witless. Clinging to the metal handrail of what looked like an indoor fire escape, I pulled my way up the impossibly tall brick wall backstage at the Music Hall. It was the mid-1980s and I was writing for a now-defunct local newspaper. It was a big story. Portsmouth, New Hampshire's last surviving downtown theater had been sold at auction and was at risk of being wrecked or gutted and turned into luxury condominiums. Thankfully, the new owners pledged to restore the aging 1878 playhouse to its former glory. I was meeting them for a tour and interview.

I have a vague memory of reaching the top of the stairs some seventy-five feet above the stage floor. Then there was a short metal ladder, a creaky wooden hatch, and a blinding light. The view of New Hampshire's only seaport was spectacular. It's true that from the roof of the Music Hall one can see all the way down the Piscataqua River to the Isles of Shoals ten miles away.

On previous assignments, I had viewed the heart of the city from the wooden steeple of the old North Church as it creaked and shuddered in the wind. I had ridden the middle span of Memorial Bridge that connects Portsmouth to Kittery, Maine, that rose like a giant elevator as a parade of tall ships glided beneath me. But I had never been as petrified as the day I stood atop the Music Hall, glanced around, and hurried back down to sea level.

Thirty-five years later, given the chance to climb the back-stage ladder again for this book, I politely declined. In her historic tours of the theater, production manager Zhana Morris points out the elaborate "fly system" of ropes, pulleys, and counter-weights that make this one of the finest theatrical venues in New England. Brave production crew members routinely scramble unseen where writers fear to tread.

OPPOSITE: *Temptations founding member Otis Williams thanks a fan from the stage. (DJM)*

"Theaters and shipbuilding have always been closely tied," Zhana said as we wandered among hulking electrical panels, past stark dressing rooms, and around theater props. The rigging team that changes the scenery or makes Peter Pan fly could be operating the sails on a tall ship, she told me. And in a Navy town like Portsmouth, there were plenty of skilled sailors, painters, carpenters, and woodcarvers to build and maintain a Victorian theater of this quality. But there were not always enough people to fill the seats.

The story of our beloved Music Hall is tidal. It ebbs and flows with popular tastes and trends in the performing arts. It shifts with the economy and with current events. It bends around the goals and resources of its many owners, and rises or falls with evolving technology. Such theaters, as this book will demonstrate, are forever at risk of disappearing. The owners who climbed the metal stairs to the roof with me back in the 1980s fell quickly into debt. Within months of its salvation the theater was back on the auction block and in danger of demolition.

At this writing I've been poring over the story of the Portsmouth landmark theater for almost two years, working through the physical and digital archives that Zhana, the official Music Hall historian, has been collecting for two decades. The first two chapters are my attempt to show how a Victorian theater evolved out of a tiny colonial seaport squashed between the expansive coastlines of Massachusetts and Maine. Music and theater, I hope to show, have been with us since the beginning.

I'm fine with the fact that this is a picture book, too. It may sit like others I have written on a coffee table for years before anyone discovers the text. I was surprised to discover the similarity between the early itinerant performers — the magicians, musicians, actors, and acrobats — and the traveling vaudeville acts that would follow. And despite a lifetime of writing about this town, I had never heard of the Cameneum, a forgotten nineteenth-century theater that has since become a parking lot.

It was fascinating during my research to watch a Baptist church that once stood on the site of the Music Hall morph into the "Temple." Over a period of sixty years, the church pulpit became a podium and then a stage. The boxy pews were replaced by curved amphitheater seating. The sermons, meanwhile, turned into temperance rallies, lyceum lectures, minstrel shows, and eventually a showcase for hypnotists and comedians. Like time-lapse photography, we can see the architecture adapt to meet the more secular desires of the ticket-buying public who wanted, increasingly, to be entertained as well as enlightened. They wanted a theater.

The Music Hall we know gets built by the Peirce family in Chapter Three of this book. Ale tycoon Frank Jones expands and beautifies the building in Chapter Four. According to one media account, Jones was almost killed when a hammer fell from high above as he was inspecting the renovated stage.

Jones died the following year anyway, and in Chapter Five the story takes us into the vaudeville and silent film era of theater owner F.W. Hartford, a Portsmouth mayor and newspaper mogul. Hartford's family scrapbook and business records are archived at the Portsmouth Athenaeum. His son Justin inherits the theater in Chapter Six and spends World War II struggling to unload the shuttered and decaying hall. Scraps of his letters are published here for the first time. Then Guy Tott of Kittery buys the building at auction for $10,000, turns it into a movie house he calls the Civic, leases it to movie mogul Elias Loew, and promptly dies.

Like untold thousands of film fans, this is where I came in. By the 1970s and '80s, with its cracked tile floors and funky bathrooms, the Civic (we called it "Old Stickyfoot") was a ghost of its former self. In Chapter Seven it almost expires. Then finally, following a series of close calls, the theater is saved in Chapter Eight by the nonprofit Friends of the Music Hall. The tide, to recover my previous metaphor, rises again, but that doesn't mean smooth sailing.

Continuing our tour of the historic building, I follow Zhana Morris down a narrow flight of stairs to a cramped cluttered workspace below the stage. From here, until the twenty-first century, there was only a solid ledge. But in Chapter Nine workers excavate 700 cubic feet of rocks to carve out space for more dressing rooms, a bar, and the wild and crazy Beaux Arts-style lobby. Its fanciful sculptural design, including two must-see lavatories, could be the interior of a Jules Verne sci-fi submarine or a forest in Tolkien's Middle-earth.

This final chapter tracks the vision of executive director Patricia Lynch who arrived in Portsmouth in 2004. Stepping through the lobby and out the swinging leather-clad doors, her vision for the theater is in full bloom. A brilliantly lit neon marquee rises above a redesigned pedestrian streetscape that leads to a towering metal arch. And there's more.

A block away at the modern Music Hall Loft, I'm greeted by Monte Bohanan, director of marketing and communications. The book is almost done, I tell him, and there are stories yet to tell. But we have no room for "The Phantom," a painted figure who appeared beneath the wallpaper during the theater's 125th anniversary jubilee. And what about Orlando the cat, who applied for the job as official theater mouser in the 1990s and was known to hop into the lap of startled movie-goers? Or the time Music Hall staffers grabbed a defibrillator and rushed to restart a woman's heart before the paramedics arrived?

"Maybe we can work them into the pictures in the book," Monte suggests. For a guy who lives in a world of crushing deadlines, Monte is surprisingly calm. Back in the 1980s, the Music Hall staged about thirty shows per year. Including the Loft, that number has hit an astonishing 600 events annually, he says. We wander past the upscale bar counter to the 120-seat Loft theater and up the stairs where an unsung band is at work behind the scenes. These are the marketing people, the development team, the programming, financial, and administrative staff. There are stage managers, box office and concession crew, projectionists, sound and lighting technicians — not to mention hundreds of volunteers, plus board members, sponsors, and thousands of Music Hall members.

And these people are not stamping out widgets. Every performance is unique. In the two years I was hunched over my computer or huddled in some quiet archive I also caught a bunch of shows.

I watched a very pregnant Natalie MacMaster dancing with her family while fiercely fiddling Cape Breton tunes. I saw the Oyster River High School band flawlessly playing the soundtrack to a Buster Keaton silent film. Where else could I shake hands with novelist Dan Brown, or catch Tinariwen, a Grammy Award-winning group of musicians from the Sahara Desert region of northern Mali? During two lively Christmas musicals, it snowed inside the theater. And it's still hard to believe I watched astronaut Scott Kelly, who spent a record-breaking year orbiting 230 miles above the Earth on the same stage where, a few weeks earlier, "Weird Al" Yankovic performed. The same stage, by the way, was once occupied by Mark Twain, John Philip Sousa, and Buffalo Bill Cody.

The tour ends at the office door of Patricia Lynch. Monte knocks. We enter. I tell her that the manuscript is done and thank her for trusting the theater's history to me. We'll start assembling the illustrations tomorrow and publish in the fall.

"How is it," I ask, "that the Music Hall team can keep up its relentless production pace?"

"You have to have tough skin to work here," Patricia says. "You need a tremendously curious mind and be willing to take on all sorts of challenges, to learn new skills all the time, be relentless on yourself and then be able to laugh. That's the Music Hall culture — ethical, transparent, real rock and roll, irreverent, and fanatical about quality. These are the things that matter to us."

Luckily, I have my tape recorder on. That's exactly the quotation I've been looking for to wrap up my Introduction to this book. I remind Patricia that, back when this project started, she described the Music Hall as a "family." It seemed like a cliché back then, I admit. Now I get it. This is show business.

What I still don't get is how this whole theater thing happens day after day, night after night. I'm exhausted just imagining the planning, the costs, the logistics — not to mention the range of human emotions evoked from those few square feet of a wooden stage for almost a century and a half. It has to be magic, we all agree. There's no other explanation. ❧

J. Dennis Robinson
2019

CHAPTER 1

Make a Joyful Noise
The performing arts in early Portsmouth

T he English settlers who started what is now Portsmouth, New Hampshire in 1630 brought along plenty of musical instruments, but only one Bible. Along with the requisite pistols, swords, and cannons for defense of the fledgling outpost, an ancient inventory lists two drums, plus "15 hautboys and soft recorders." A hautboy (pronounced "o-boy") was a seventeenth-century oboe — a tuneful, easy-to-play, and compact instrument, ideal for the 3,000 mile journey to the fearsome wilderness of the New World. While the two drums were for military training, one local historian notes, the oboes and recorders had the emotive power "to cheer the immigrants in their solitude."

Linking a few woodwinds that arrived here aboard a wooden ship to the story of the Music Hall centuries later may be a stretch, but there is much here to unpack. Portsmouth historians have long argued that, unlike the pious Pilgrims of Plymouth Plantation, our founders came to catch fish, to plant crops, to fell trees, to trade with the Natives, and to search for precious metals. And when the long workday was over, they wanted to unwind.

The evidence of that single Bible in the inventory, and the fact that it took years for Portsmouth colonists to hire their first minister tugs at the myth that America was settled by men and women in search of religious freedom. A few certainly were. But the history of the Piscataqua River region, like much of the nation, is really about commerce, risk, and survival. New

ABOVE: *A 1726 treble viol. (MET)*
OPPOSITE: *Willian Hogarth's comic engraving* The Enraged Musician *(1741) depicts a violinist distracted by the street noise outside his window. One man is playing a "hautboy" or early oboe like the first musical instruments imported by the early English settlers at Strawberry Bank, now Portsmouth, New Hampshire. (WIK)*

Hampshire's predominantly English founders wanted land, wealth, and independence.

As Portsmouth (originally called "Strawberry Bank") was getting off to a rocky start, more than 20,000 English people migrated to the New World, especially to nearby Massachusetts, in search of the same land, wealth, and independence. Some moved north to escape restrictive Puritan laws and exclusive religious practices, and were welcomed into the wild and woolly Piscataqua River region. To Puritan leader John Winthrop, the Strawberry Bank settlement was a lawless area that sheltered religious outlaws and "lewd persons." In 1628, for example, when lawyer Thomas Morton was discovered dancing around a maypole and partying with Native Americans in Massachusetts, he was kidnapped from his home by religious purists, dragged aboard a ship, and abandoned ten miles off the New Hampshire coast at the isolated Isles of Shoals. Morton was rescued, he later reported, due to the kindness of local Indians and traveling fishermen.

For much of the 1600s, the Puritans exercised military and legal control over New Hampshire, but unlike Maine and Massachusetts, Portsmouth retained much of its unique personality. That personality evolved in the 1700s, as we will see, when New Hampshire became a separate and commercially successful royal colony with close ties to the English kings. As New Hampshire's only seaport and an important hub of maritime trade, Portsmouth was also the heart of local politics, arts, and culture.

For reasons we will explore, Portsmouth came to embrace its reputation as a party town. Nineteenth-century writers like Eliza Buckminster Lee, the daughter of an influential Portsmouth minister, pictured the city as a sort of anti-Massachusetts.

"Puritanism had little in forming the character of Portsmouth," she wrote in 1848. "[The people] were little given to days of fasting and prayer . . . Indeed, in almost all celebrations of public events, instead of a sermon, there was a ball; instead of days of fasting in Portsmouth, all public demonstrations of feeling ended with a feast."

ABOVE: *Puritan lawyer John Winthrop (1587/8-1649), a founder and governor of the Massachusetts Bay Colony, saw the Piscataqua as a lawless region willing to shelter "all such lewd persons" who fled from Puritan rule. (AAS/WIK)*

Music in the air

Scattered documents and artifacts do not bring Portsmouth's first century back to life. Our surviving first period structures, the Sherburne House (1695) at Strawbery Banke Museum and the Jackson House (1664) can only hint at the harsh lifestyle of their colonial inhabitants. With almost no pictures and few documents of that era we are left listening to the frontier sounds of crying wolves, crashing waves, moaning oxen, and the rhythmic whine of a distant sawmill.

That's a shame, because our first planters, adventurers, and fishermen must have been a raucous bunch. They were products of the so-called English Renaissance, an age when poetry, drama, art, and song flourished. William Shakespeare was dead, but playwrights Ben Jonson and George Chapman were still alive and the second Globe Theatre in London was still open when the original Portsmouth settlers left their homeland. They left a world echoing with madrigals, chorales, and chamber music. Many had grown up within the traditions of the Church of England that allowed "a genial patronage of gaiety and merriment." Local historian John Scribner Jenness reminds us that the settlers at Strawberry Bank were happily familiar with "maypoles,

ABOVE: *Now owned and managed by Historic New England, the 1664-era Jackson House in Portsmouth is the oldest surviving wood-frame house in New Hampshire. (SBM)*

LEFT: *Immigrants to the New World, English Puritans included, brought along their lively music and dances. This early–1620s watercolor by Dutch artist Adriaen van de Venne depicts a peasant couple dancing. (BMC)*

morris dances, wassails, and junketings of all sorts." It is unthinkable that our European ancestors left their sea chanties, bawdy tavern drinking songs, or country dancing behind in England. A growing population of enslaved men and women also brought their traditional dances, rituals, and songs from Africa to the Piscataqua shores.

Lacking a time machine, we cannot prove music filled the salty air along the Piscataqua in the seventeenth century. The first book published in British North America, however, was a Puritan hymnal that translated the Old Testament psalms into "singable" English poems. The Bay Psalm Book was printed at Cambridge, Massachusetts in 1640. It is possible that one or more of the 1,700 original copies made their way to the Puritan dominated New Hampshire towns of Exeter, Hampton, and Dover, or even to the less pious settlers at Portsmouth. So check your attic. A rare surviving copy of the Bay Psalm Book sold at auction a few years ago for over $14 million.

Scholar Louis Pichierri combed through countless early New Hampshire documents searching for references to musical instruments. In 1688, for example, a Hampton resident listed a trumpet in his will, most likely for military use. Portsmouth merchant John Shipway bequeathed a "treble viol" to his heirs. Around this time, a London lawyer staying at an inn on nearby Great Island (now New Castle), noted the following in his journal: "In the evening, as soon as I had supped in the outer room before mine, I took a little musical instrument and began to touch it." The reference to "touch," Louis Pichierri explains, probably means the guest at the tavern was strumming a borrowed lute.

Adventurer John Josselyn, who toured the Piscataqua in the 1660s offered this rare observation of Native Americans making their own stringed instruments by hand and playing them on the nearby Maine coast:

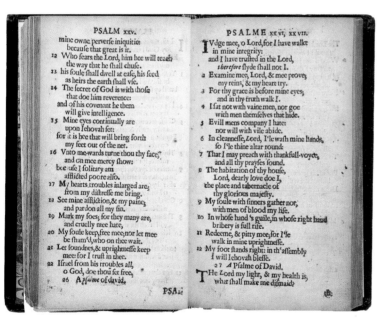

ABOVE: *The first book published in British North America,* The Bay Psalm Book *was printed at Cambridge, Massachusetts, in 1640.* (MIS)

Musical too they be . . . but instruments they had none before the English came amongst them. Since, they have imitated them and will make 'Kitts' and string them as neatly and as artifically (*sic*) as the best fiddle maker amongst us, and will play our plain lessons very exactly. The only fiddler that was in the province of Maine, when I was there, was an Indian called Scozway, whom the fisherman and planters — when they had a mind to be merry — made use of.

The governor and the Assembly House

Three wealthy men set the stage very early for Portsmouth to become a modern cultural destination. Credit goes first to Captain John Mason of Portsmouth, England, the "founding father" of New Hampshire. Mason and his fellow investors hoped to install a profitable British trading post on the Piscataqua River. The Strawberry Bank experiment, however, was a financial flop. The investment company shut down and Mason died in 1635 without ever seeing his colony. Although abandoned in the New World by its backers, Strawberry Bank, soon renamed Portsmouth, managed to survive.

King Charles II takes second prize for making Portsmouth unique. It was Charles who turned New Hampshire into a separate royal province in 1679. By doing so, the King of England drove a tiny Royalist wedge between Puritan holdings in Maine and Massachusetts, creating a major British tradeport.

Third prize goes to Royal Governor Benning Wentworth whose opulent lifestyle transformed Portsmouth into a tiny copy of the British aristocracy. Local historians tend to picture Benning Wentworth as the portly, gouty, elderly governor who, at age sixty-four, married his twenty-three-year-old housekeeper, Martha Hilton. But his twenty-five-year reign, beginning in 1741, also ushered in an economic boom as Portsmouth became a world trading center. The governor issued lucrative land grants and set up towns as far away as Bennington, Vermont, carving out 500 acres in each new township for himself, and spreading the wealth among cronies and relatives.

ABOVE: *Born in Portsmouth, New Hampshire's Royal Governor Benning Wentworth (1696-1770) and his wealthy friends and relatives pursued a lifestyle in imitation of the British gentry. (NHH/ATH)*

Born in Portsmouth in 1696, one of thirteen children, Benning Wentworth was a mediocre student and hell-raiser at Harvard College, where he held the undergraduate record for breaking the most windows. Like his father John Wentworth, New Hampshire's lieutenant governor, Benning started out in the merchant trade. He was well-travelled and rubbed shoulders with the English gentry. As he prospered, Portsmouth partied.

The privileged life of the Wentworth and other Portsmouth families enthralled many nineteenth- and twentieth-century writers including Mary Cochran Rogers of Boston. Her book, *Glimpses of an Old Social Capital* (1923), chronicles the elite residents of Portsmouth. Rogers does not acknowledge the sizable population of enslaved Africans, who often lived and worked in the same households. Here Rogers describes the Sunday parade of parishioners leaving the Anglican church of Rev. Arthur Browne in Portsmouth:

BELOW: *Late nineteenth century actors dressed in eighteenth century costumes for a local production. Cast members include John Templeman Coolidge Jr., whose Boston family summered in the Benning Wentworth mansion at Little Harbor. (ATH)*

At the door of Queen's Chapel were chariots with liveried footman behind, waiting for the gentry to come out. First the gentlemen — wearing immense wigs white as snow, coats trimmed with gold lace, embroidered waistcoats, ruffles of delicate lace, silk stockings, gold buckles at knee and shoe, three-cornered hats, and carrying gold-headed canes — and now the ladies come forth, stately, powdered, with exquisite lace handkerchiefs folded over brocade dresses or rare and beautiful mantles from overseas — and when they were seated, the pageant passed on.

The Portsmouth elite had their portraits painted by important artists like Joseph Blackburn and possibly John Singleton Copley. They preferred fine food, drank the best imported liquor, and lived in elegant homes. They were also fond of music, fine art, new books, live theater, dancing, horse racing, card playing, and other things that offended many pious New Englanders. In nearby Boston, the sporting life of the rich and famous was considered a threat to the morality and livelihood of the less fortunate. So in 1750, Boston's city fathers banned all stage-plays, interludes, and other theatrical entertainments.

The Boston theater ban, following a religious "Great Awakening" that swept through New England, must have dampened Portsmouth's party vibe. One local minister, writing to a colleague, claimed "vices that have been usual in a seaport" were on the wane. Dancing and music seemed to be "wholly laid aside," he observed, while "profane and obscene songs" were being replaced by righteous hymns and psalms.

The minister was either bending the truth or not paying close attention. In 1750, the very year of the Boston theater ban, a small, red-faced man named Michael Whidden opened the Assembly House on Vaughan Street, now Vaughan Mall in downtown Portsmouth. The stately white building had three great parlors and a kitchen on the first floor. An immense stairway opened onto a huge second floor hall measuring thirty by sixty feet with tall windows and three chandeliers lit with wax candles. All but forgotten today, the Assembly House with its gilded wood carvings became the entertainment center for the

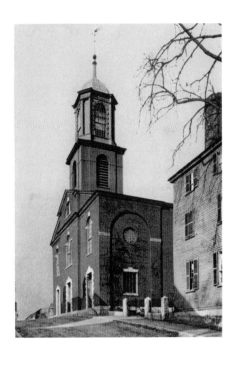

ABOVE: *An early postcard view of St. John's Church on Chapel Street. The original 1732 building, known as Queen's Chapel, was visited by President George Washington in 1789. Destroyed in the fire of 1806, the Anglican church was rebuilt the following year. Gov. Benning Wentworth and other Portsmouth notables are buried in the churchyard here. (ATH)*

ABOVE: *A highly imagined view of the colonial era Assembly House, site of Vaughan Mall today, by twentieth-century painter Harry S. Harlow. Enslaved African musicians Prince and Cuffee Whipple were frequent performers at gala events held here. (PHS)*

city's upper crust, and eventually the next best thing to a public playhouse.

Supported by wealthy subscribers, Whidden's hall offered eight gala winter dances annually. Bejeweled ladies in low-cut dresses of silk and satin, their hair adorned with ostrich feathers, were escorted up to the ballroom by uniformed managers. Gentlemen followed, dressed in fashionable blue coats with shiny buttons, plus "knee breeches, silk stockings, pumps, and white kid gloves." Everyone joined in the public "draw dances," taking their place according to assigned numbers. Eighteenth-century French-style cotillion dancing, however, was more challenging, and therefore voluntary. Brave couples attempted the minuet and other popular European steps while encircled by hundreds of admiring and sometimes critical spectators, an early version of *Dancing with the Stars.* During intermission, guests ate delicate

sandwiches of tongue or ham, drank lemonade, and were served spiced chocolate by an enslaved African cook.

In 1762 Benning Wentworth received a petition requesting permission for an itinerant actor "to erect a play-house here sometime hence." The 47 signers — with names like Atkinson, Livermore, Warner, and Rindge — were largely from the city's upper class. Two counter petitions followed, signed by a total of 223 citizens who opposed the idea of a Portsmouth theater. Echoing the sentiments of the Boston theater ban, the conservatives argued that "such Liberty would great (*sic*) effect the interest as well as morals of the people."

The aging governor Wentworth was in a tough spot following his scandalous marriage to Martha Hilton just two years prior. His nepotism and sketchy financial dealings were gaining public attention, even as he and his second wife occupied a sprawling mansion at Little Harbor with over forty rooms. George III, who was soon to enact a series of hated colonial taxes, was the new king of England. All this came in the summer of a devastating drought and a struggling economy. So Benning Wentworth, despite his love of the latest English culture, let the theater petition die. Five years later, with revolutionary protest in the air, Benning passed the royal governorship to his handsome and popular nephew John Wentworth.

ABOVE: *The seacoast hub of early theatrical entertainments, dances, concerts, classes, traveling shows, and exhibitions, the Assembly House faded with the arrival of Franklin Hall built nearby in the early 1800s. The central hall of the Assembly House was removed and the building divided into two separate tenements, creating what was then Raitts Court between the two halves. These buildings were demolished in the early 1970s. (ATH)*

Say you want a Revolution

Tracking the rise of the arts in Portsmouth gets a little easier with the appearance of the *New Hampshire Gazette* in 1756. We see by the following year that merchant Robert Trail had imported the "best Italian violin strings." The *Gazette,* and briefly the *New Hampshire Spy,* offered advertisements for plays, concerts, lectures, exhibits, classes, and, as we will soon discover, an array of "lewd amusements."

In 1767, as John Wentworth took office and the hated Stamp Act was repealed, Mr. Peter Curtis began placing advertisements for dancing and violin lessons. The new governor, like his uncle, was fond of music and dancing. We know because he was, even then, building a grand summer mansion in the wilds of Wolfeboro, New Hampshire, with a forty-foot-long ballroom. Wentworth wrote to a friend in England seeking to import two indentured servants who could play the violin or French horn. The musicians would be given fine clothes, Wentworth promised, and after five years service, they could receive up to one hundred acres of good New Hampshire land. It did not matter, Wentworth wrote, what country the men came from or what religion they followed. Nor did they have to be first-rate musicians, he added, since "we are not great connoisseurs in that way."

Despite the lack of a formal playhouse and the lingering influence of the Boston theater ban, dramatic and comic stage productions were creeping into town. In 1765 the newspaper noted tickets on sale for a production of *The Beggar's Opera* at an unspecified venue. Then in 1769, the year Gov. Wentworth created his summer mansion, an actor billed as "Mr. Douglas" delivered a "Lecture on Heads" at John Stavers' newly built tavern, then known as The Earl of Halifax, on present day Court Street. This strange and little known "curtain lecture," launched in London in 1764, became a turning point in the evolution of theater in America.

The "Lecture on Heads" was a comedic performance disguised as a moral and educational talk. The English originator, George Alexander Stevens, opened the show by placing fifty papier mâché heads on a table spread with a green cloth. The heads, some wearing wigs or hats, represented different

ABOVE: *Portsmouth-born and beloved until the rise of the American Revolution, Gov. John Wentworth (1737-1820) was fond of dancing, music, and theater. Exiled from New Hampshire in 1775, he later became Lieutenant-Governor of Nova Scotia.*
(HMA/WIK)

characters. Employing props, songs, poems, different voices and accents, Stevens displayed and satirized each head — a preacher, an old maid, a judge, a quack doctor — in a nonstop two-hour monologue. The Portsmouth lecture in Stavers' tavern was likely tame by comparison. And it was definitely based on a pirated version of the London original. It was decades before Stephens published a heavily illustrated manual on his popular

ABOVE: *First performed in London in 1764, a "Lecture on Heads" satirized popular fashion and personalities. After a rousing success in Great Britain, playwright-actor-songwriter George Alexander Stevens (1710-1780) brought his theatrical comedy to America. (JDR)*

show, complete with instructions on satirizing each character. But despite claims that the "Lecture on Heads" was moral and educational, it was theater through and through.

In the fall of 1772, as the American Revolution loomed, a Boston musician and teacher, W.S. Morgan, began offering "weekly exhibitions" at the Oratorical Academy Room at what was certainly Stavers' Tavern. Morgan's five-person crew delivered a medley of prologues, songs, dances, pantomimes, and short dramatic readings. As they had done a decade earlier, Portsmouth officials complained. "It is against the minds of the Town," they argued, "that Mr. Morgan or any other person, exhibit plays or any other shows in this town." But Morgan's troupe continued for several months, marking 1772 as the port city's first theatrical season.

The show was over, however, for the Wentworth dynasty. On December 13, 1774, urged on by a visit from Paul Revere, the good citizens of Portsmouth and surrounding towns raided King George III's fort at New Castle. They stole weapons and carried away as many as a hundred kegs of gunpowder. Early the next year, the once-beloved Gov. John Wentworth, his wife Frances, and their infant son were driven from their home on Pleasant Street and exiled from New Hampshire, never to return under penalty of death.

Drums of war

The rat-a-tat of military drums has always been part of the Portsmouth soundtrack. Drumbeats urged brave local men to board ships in 1745 and sail to Nova Scotia to oppose the French at Fort Louisbourg. Many never returned. At the repeal of the Stamp Act in 1766, according to the *NH Gazette*, "the bells rang an incessant peal, drums and music contributed to make the harmony of sounds concordant to the apparent temper and disposition of the people." Drummers roused the locals into their treasonous raid on the King's fort at New Castle and convinced men to risk life and limb on land and at sea.

Andrew Sherburne, who signed on as a Portsmouth privateer at age thirteen, later recalled the pulsing power of military drums

ABOVE: *Characters from a "Lecture on Heads" performed in Portsmouth as early as 1769.*
(JDR)

at the outbreak of the American Revolution. The bustle of ships in the harbor, sounds of soldiers training in the fields, and flags waving was intoxicating to a young boy. "The roar of cannon," Sherburne wrote in his memoir, "the sound of martial music and the call for volunteers so infatuated me, that I was filled with anxiety to become an actor in the scene of war."

The theater, with one exception, disappeared from the port city during the American Revolution. Many of the wealthy Loyalists who had lobbied for a Portsmouth playhouse were now gone, exiled to England or to Canada like ex-governor John Wentworth. Itinerant actors, with no work, sat out the war in the West Indies. A rare exception was a production of Shakespeare's

ABOVE: *Originally entitled* Yankee Doodle *this patriotic painting by Archibald MacNeal Willard is best known as* The Spirit of '76. *The original hangs in Abbot Hall in Marblehead, Massachusetts. (WIK)*

tragedy *Coriolanus,* performed by the crewman aboard a ship moored at Portsmouth Harbor in 1778. Four years later naval hero John Paul Jones, having returned to Portsmouth after his famous attack on the British Isles, reportedly sponsored a party on the decks of the warship *America* being built at Kittery, complete with dancing and fireworks.

With the war against King George III almost won, a band of French musicians delivered a concert at a Portsmouth shipyard. The following year in 1783 the drum call to battle gave way to the beat of victory in countless parades. Patriotic celebrations have marked every Fourth of July since. Upon hearing that the U.S. Constitution had been ratified in 1788, a group of musicians piled into a horse-drawn coach and erupted in joyous songs as their carriage wound through the narrow streets of Portsmouth.

Experiment in theater

Following the heady thrill of victory, Portsmouth quickly went back to being Portsmouth, including a return to the elite ballroom parties at the Assembly House. The city's aristocratic families, those who had wisely shifted to the Patriot cause, danced once again to the fiddle music of Prince and Cuffee Whipple, two talented African performers who played in the balcony above the white guests. Prince, enslaved by William Whipple, Portsmouth's heralded signer of the Declaration of Independence, had joined other black men of New Hampshire in petitioning for his own freedom in the new United States. That petition was ignored. The African musicians were sometimes joined by Col. Michael Wentworth, the second husband of Martha Hilton, and a cousin of her late husband, Gov. Benning Wentworth. An enthusiastic amateur musician, Michael Wentworth frequently left their rambling Little Harbor mansion to jam until all hours with the Whipple brothers.

The most famous guest at the Assembly House was none other than President George Washington, who spent four days in Portsmouth during his post-election tour in the fall of 1789. Washington, who enjoyed near godlike status, arrived in town to a

ABOVE: *Naval hero John Paul Jones (1747-1792) lodged in Portsmouth twice during the American Revolution while fitting out the warships* Ranger *and* America. *The John Paul Jones House Museum (built 1758) operated by the Portsmouth Historical Society is adjacent to the Music Hall on Porter Street, formerly Prison Lane. (JDR)*

cheering throng, singing children, ringing bells, blasting cannon, marching bands, and a rousing chorus of "Hail Columbia."

Washington's visit was a musical theater production in itself. The nation's first president heard sacred songs at both Queen's Chapel, conveniently renamed St. John's, and at the Congregational North Church in Market Square. When President Washington took a boat tour of Portsmouth Harbor, a number of young musicians, dressed in white frocks and "anxious to afford our illustrious and beloved president all the entertainment in their power," followed in a barge and serenaded Washington as he fished for cod in the Piscataqua River. The next day, Washington penned this entry in his journal:

> About 2 o'clock I rec'd an Address from the Executive of the State of New Hampshire; and in half an hour after dined with them and a large Company at their Assembly room which is one of the best I have seen anywhere in the United States. At half after Seven I went to the Assembly where there were about 75 well dressed, and many of them very handsome Ladies.

With the Boston theater ban still in effect, the Assembly House and a few Portsmouth taverns were becoming semi-legitimate stages. The same year as Washington's visit, the Assembly House presented *The Better Sort*, a "ballad opera" in

ABOVE: *During his four-day visit to Portsmouth in 1789, President George Washington attended a dance at the Assembly House that he called "one of the best [assembly rooms] I have seen anywhere in the United States." This 1929 canvas in the collection of the Virginia Historical Society depicts Washington dancing in celebration of the victory at Yorktown in 1781. (WIK)*

which the heroine rejects Alonzo Hazard and marries Harry Truelove. The performance included a plea to bring back public theater, because satire contained the power to "reform the age."

The idea that the theater, rather than being a source of moral corruption to society, was possibly a source of moral improvement was gaining momentum. A recent émigré from Nova Scotia to Portsmouth, Andrew Halliburton, had much to say on the topic. A customs official by trade, Halliburton would become one of the city's most respected scholars and lyceum speakers in the coming century. His essay, "The Effects of the Stage on the Manners of a People," theorized that a "virtuous theater" had the ability to "impel, direct or restrain the spirits of a nation!"

"It is generally acknowledged," Halliburton wrote, "that a well-written play, well performed and assisted by good and appropriate scenery, is the most fascinating of all mental enjoyments, especially to the young and imaginative."

Theater, therefore, was a powerful tool. Moralists who attempted to destroy theaters, like the puritanical Bostonians, were missing the point. A good theater managed by the right people could purify the minds of Americans. It is an argument that has been applied to every entertainment medium, from books to cinema, and from television to the internet. The government, according to Halliburton, should control the theater to keep it virtuous. Using satire, the government could then expose the "follies and absurdities" of modern society and "purify the mind" of each audience member. Such power, Halliburton warned, should not fall into the hands of commercial men who would make a profit, rather than reform the country.

By 1790, with a population hovering around 5,000, Portsmouth was at its economic peak. But with the state capital transferred to Exeter for safety during the Revolution (and later to Concord) Portsmouth had lost its political clout even as New Hampshire was expanding. The profitable mast and lumber trade that had made the Wentworths a fortune was moving to cheaper alternative ports like Newburyport, Salem, Saco, and Boston. Things would get worse long before they got better.

"The traveler is always disappointed when he visits Portsmouth," a letter to the *NH Gazette* proclaimed.

ABOVE: *An actor pelted with fruit, copied from a collection of essays by Portsmouth-born humorist Benjamin Penhallow Shillaber.*
(JDR)

Instead of a large well-built city, he finds a town out of repair, without elegant public buildings and institutions, and with few well-built private dwellings: like a family once great and wealthy, the inhabitants appear great by repeating what they were once.

There were plenty of billiard tables in Portsmouth in 1790, the visitor noted, but no respectable college or academy. The inhabitants, nostalgic for the city's glory days, seemed to pass their time attending balls, feasts, recitals, tea parties, and picnics. Or they were gathered at the Assembly House taking lessons in dancing, singing, drawing, playing musical instruments, painting miniature portraits, and speaking French.

It was into this entertainment-obsessed society that the city's first theater was about to open late in the final weeks of 1791. A band of local literary gentlemen, aged twenty to twenty-five, were renovating a warehouse on Bow Street and fitting out a stage. Mr. Civil, who taught many of the classes at the Assembly House, and a Mr. Gannet were the principals. According to the *New Hampshire Spy,* subscriptions were pouring in for a season of eight performances.

The first show, featuring an all-male amateur cast, was a popular London comedy entitled *The West Indian.* J.M. Sewall, a noted Portsmouth lawyer and poet, reminded viewers it had been barely fifteen years, with "wealth exhausted [and] seas of gore," since America had won her independence from Britain. In his prologue to the play Sewall promised only the "chastest scenes" would follow. Remembered as a sickly and nervous fellow, Sewall reinforced Andrew Halliburton's reformist thesis that "pleasure joining with improvement" was good medicine for everyone. In the upcoming satire, Sewall proclaimed:

The sufferer shall be cheered,
Inspired the brave,
The coxcomb ridiculed.
And lashed the knave.

Reviews of the Bow Street Theater were mixed as the 1792 season worked through a catalog of satirical British plays including *Miss in Her Teens, The Lying Valet,* and *The Absent*

ABOVE: *A dueling scene from the British farce* Miss in Her Teens *was staged at the short-lived Portsmouth theater on Bow Street in the late eighteenth century. (BMC/WIK)*

Wife along with pantomime and musical interludes. Historian Charles Brewster reminds us that, as in Shakespeare's day, "the most delicate young men, in flowing robes and curls, personified the ladies." There was even brief competition from a five-person acting troupe, including two married couples, who gave a few shows at the Assembly House. Their leader, an Englishman named Mr. Watts, was characterized in the newspaper as "a vulgar fellow with a wry neck."

It was, by all accounts, a rough season. Unruly young men without tickets snuck in from behind the scenery. Others tossed chestnuts and apples onto the stage. The actors, according to a letter in the newspaper, "drink spirituous liquors in order to keep up their strength." Most complaints, however, came from citizens already opposed to the theater. Conservatives argued that moral plays could never be enacted by drunken and immoral people, who, by definition, all actors were. *The Spy*, although a supporter of the theater, published a letter by a man who was "besotted" with the playhouse until "God awakened me with his thunder." The writer, who had overcome his addiction to the theater through Christian prayer, hoped he might save others from the "fatal" lure of such seductive amusements.

The little theater in the Bow Street warehouse was ahead of its time. Not even the new scenery for a presentation of *The Grecian Daughter* could save it. The painted backdrops, the newspaper announced, included a ship leaving the harbor, an escape from the jaws of a sea monster, and a chariot drawn by seahorses. And not even the presence of the wife and family of New Hampshire governor Josiah Bartlett, another signer of the Declaration of Independence, could help. Nor could the poetic pleas of J.M. Sewall, who described the converted warehouse as an "infant stage by pious zealots cursed." By summer, with too few subscriptions to fund another season, Portsmouth's first theater failed. The stage turned back into a "paltry store" stacked with barrels, boxes, and bales. The warehouse burned in 1806 and the theater soon passed from memory.

Sacred and profane

It was John Hancock, the man with the boldest signature on the Declaration of Independence, who helped instigate the Boston theater ban in 1750. But by 1792, when Hancock, then governor of Massachusetts, tried to enforce his unpopular law, the public rioted. Hancock died the following year and, as if in celebration, Boston's first playhouse, the Federal Street Theatre, opened for business. Boston quickly became the theater hub of New England. Portsmouth took its place among other "circuit towns," like Salem, Portland, and Newburyport, that regularly hosted traveling actors based in Boston. As we shall see, the three-day Music Hall premiere in 1878 was staged entirely by a Boston theater company. Back in the 1790s, however, Boston was still a bone-jarring, fifteen-hour stagecoach ride from Portsmouth, so itinerant entertainers were enthusiastically welcomed here.

It would be a mistake to stereotype Portsmouth as merely a rough and tumble party town. Portsmouth played, but it also prayed and sang. The church singing in seventeenth-century Strawberry Bank was primitive, and probably followed the traditional "lining out" of hymns. Church elders, at first, sang a line

ABOVE: *Declaration of Independence-signer John Hancock (1737-1793) also served as governor of the Commonwealth of Massachusetts. In his declining years he issued a ban on stage plays, interludes, and lewd entertainments disguised as "moral lectures." Hancock's efforts to punish "aliens and foreigners" who tried to thwart his theater ban led to a Boston riot in 1792. (MHS/WIK)*

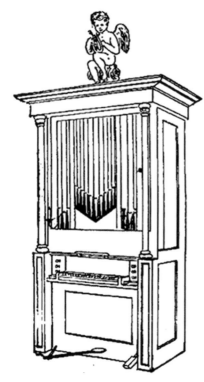

from the official psalm book. Then the congregation, unaccompanied by instruments, sang the line back, an age-old practice still followed in the isolated Scottish Hebrides. With no precise melody or fixed rhythm, individuals sang from the heart at their own pace and tune. "Lining out" a lengthy psalm might keep the congregation standing for up to half an hour.

"There must have been pockets of sameness in the room," says Jeff Warner, a Portsmouth folk singer and musicologist, "with strong singers leading the weak ones, but nothing uniform. It must have been great to be in the middle of, but not so great to listen to."

Criticism of this "wild unbridled" church music, Warner says, naturally led to the many Portsmouth singing schools of the eighteenth and nineteenth centuries, beginning with classes at the Assembly House. Traveling teachers offered lessons in harmony and musical notation. Their arrival led to singing societies and to "pew singing," where the best singers sat up front, filling churches with sonorous psalms and harmonious hymns. This practice developed into church choirs and public concerts. Published music appeared in downtown bookstores as pianos, organs, and other instruments were imported to New England.

As with the first "hautboys" shipped to Strawberry Bank, we can trace the evolution of Portsmouth music by the arrival of more sophisticated instruments. Amateur musician Michael Wentworth, for example, owned an eight-foot-long harpsichord made of rosewood and mahogany. A petite piano built in London around 1763 now resides at the Portsmouth Historical Society. St. John's Episcopal Church on Chapel Street boasts what could be the nation's oldest playable pipe organ. This rare and fully restored "Brattle organ" came from England before 1708. It served at Harvard College and in Newburyport, Massachusetts, before being installed at Portsmouth in 1836.

Ministers named Arthur Browne, Samuel Haven, and Joseph Buckminster wielded considerable influence over the port city in the eighteenth century. But so did Portsmouth tavern owners named John Stavers and James Stoodley, whose patrons came to drink, to socialize, and to be entertained. Both innkeepers, though Loyalists at heart, found it expedient during the War for Independence to switch over to the Patriot cause. Both

ABOVE: *New Hampshire's oldest piano at the Portsmouth Historical Society and an illustration of the ancient "Brattle" organ at St. John's Episcopal Church. (JDR)*

men kept enslaved African servants and hosted slave auctions. Local legends claim that John Stavers' tavern, site of the famous "Lecture on Heads," later hosted Gen. John Sullivan and the Marquis de Lafayette. James Stoodley's tavern was the site of a secret meeting with Paul Revere that incited the famous New Castle raid. Both restored buildings are part of Strawbery Banke Museum today.

So it comes as no surprise that these unruly taverns and the Assembly House became the center of "lewd amusements" introduced by traveling actors during the high tide of Portsmouth's maritime economy. By eighteenth-century definition, lewd shows were not so titillating or sexual as they were vulgar, lowbrow, or just plain ignorant. Newspaper ads from the 1790s and early 1800s, however, are full of them. They include Samuel Jameson Maginnis, a talented young puppeteer and actor, who brought his army of "Artificial Wax-Work Comedians" to town in the fall of

ABOVE: *Once located on Daniel Street, the "King's Arms" was home to James Stoodley, his family, and two enslaved African servants. Renamed Stoodley's Tavern, the historic building was moved to Hancock Street in 1966 and restored as the Education Center and offices at Strawbery Banke Museum. (SBM)*

1795. His three-and-a-half-foot-tall marionettes danced robotic jigs and hornpipes in imitation of mechanical animated figures popular in Europe.

On the chilly afternoon of February 18, 1796, a crowd gathered outside the Assembly House to witness French balloonist Jean-Pierre Blanchard's "Aerostatic Experiment." His balloon, made from 150 yards of silk taffeta and inflated to a height of twenty-three feet, rose slowly above the rooftops of Portsmouth. Blanchard, who had flown across the English Channel, was not aboard. A wicker basket dangling from the balloon carried a dog, and perhaps a cat, pig, or goat. The spectators were "very well satisfied" when the animals parachuted safely back to earth along a wire. Blanchard died in 1808 during a flight over Holland when he suffered a heart attack in mid-air and fell more than fifty feet from one of his balloons.

Also in 1796 citizens thrilled to the acrobatics of Don Pedro Clori. Blindfolded and pretending to be a drunkard, Don Pedro danced the Spanish fandango around thirteen eggs without cracking a single shell. Another strange act, Mr. Maison's mechanical and "artificial beings," were "the most astonishing productions of art that America has ever witnessed," the broadside announced. Maison toured the United States demonstrating a mysterious "self-driving carriage." Another acrobat known as Mr. Spinacutta walked the tightrope amid a fireworks display. A troupe of Boston actors guaranteed their comic antics as "an antidote for the spleen." And the acts kept coming.

Roswell Moultharp's exhibition featured twenty wax figures, including biblical characters and a likeness of President John Adams. A new newspaper, the *Portsmouth Oracle*, announced a rare chance to witness "the astonishing Invisible Lady, the Acoustic Temple & Incomprehensible Crystal." This elaborate contraption installed at Capt. Whidden's Assembly House was an optical and audio illusion. Hidden metal ducts allowed a woman secreted in another room to respond to questions posed by the audience.

And then there were animals, including Mr. Selenka's "Knowing Dog," followed a few years later by the much acclaimed

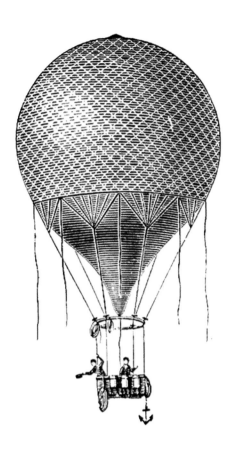

ABOVE: *Among the itinerant "lewd amusements" presented in post-Revolutionary Portsmouth was the flight of a hot air balloon in 1796 and display of a docile caged lion (left) as advertised in the* NH Gazette. *(JDR)*

"Pig of Knowledge." Both pig and dog had been scrupulously trained to pick up cards, when cued by their trainers, that made them appear to spell out words and solve mathematical problems. There were appearances by an elephant, a large male moose, and at least two lions. An eleven-year-old, 500-pound, dun-colored African lion could be seen in a sturdy cage outside Stavers' Tavern. "The person who has the care of him," according to the *NH Gazette*, "can comb his mane, make him lie down and get up at any time." Tickets were on sale daily (except on Sundays) for a fee of nine pence.

ABOVE: *The wondrously strange animals exhibited to the public for a small fee included a large moose, a small elephant, and a "Learned Pig" that could reportedly answer questions and do mathematical calculations. (JDR)*

While promoters promised only moral and upright shows, the public appetite for the unique, the bizarre, even the macabre seemed to be growing. A dwarf was on display at one tavern, an albino at another. In 1799, as the nation mourned the late George Washington, a visiting "circus" featured feats of trick horsemanship. The show was the harbinger of an early-nineteenth-century traveling menagerie that introduced Portsmouth to "unicorns," panthers, two-headed lambs, zebras, and zebu cattle, plus "infant orators," singing midgets, and a display of mummified corpses.

One final act deserves our full attention. In 1800 the upstairs "Assembly Hall" was "fitted out" as a theater with stage and seating. Three years later, in September 1803, the hall featured a performance by the famed Italian tightrope walker Signor Manfredi. A rare surviving Portsmouth broadside notes that, in

BELOW: *A rare poster now at the American Antiquarian Society announced the arrival in Portsmouth of famed tightrope walker Signor Manfredi. He was accompanied by a young Richard Potter, a black magician and ventriloquist later dubbed "America's first celebrity." Potter and his wife returned to the city often during a long career. (AAS)*

ABOVE: *Among his many talents, magician Richard Potter was able to throw his voice around the room creating the sounds of wild animals and invisible children. (JDR)*

addition to Manfredi's act, "A person of this town will perform a number of feats on the rope, with the balance pole." That person was almost certainly a young Richard Potter, the son of an enslaved woman and a white father. Potter, recent research indicates, had trained with Manfredi in Europe, but was then working as a "polite waiter" at the Portsmouth Hotel on Water Street (now Marcy Street).

Richard Potter would become the nation's first native-born ventriloquist and magician. We can hardly imagine the hard life of an itinerant African American performer in an age before trains, before electricity, before emancipation, and largely without formal theaters. Despite these difficulties, the much celebrated Mr. Potter toured widely, accompanied by his wife Sally. They did not, as one reporter claimed, toss a ball of yarn into the air in the middle of a New Hampshire field, then climb up the dangling string into the sky and disappear. But Potter could balance plates, silverware, chairs, tables, eggs, knives, and swords while teetering on a slack wire. A master of misdirection in an era hungry for entertainment, he made playing cards vanish and reappear across the room. The ventriloquist filled the hall with the magical sounds of singing birds, howling animals, and crying children.

Potter played Portsmouth at least six times over three decades as the once prominent seaport began its economic decline. Three downtown fires, all during the Christmas holiday, took their toll. The blaze of 1802 devastated Daniel Street and Market Square. The second fire in 1806 tore up Bow Street and Market Street toward the barely recovered city center. The third and worst fire in 1813 took out 300 buildings along State Street, flattening the city like a tornado. The War of 1812 further crippled the once grand colonial capital and its many sister ports.

With the grand old Assembly House also in decline, Potter and other traveling performers moved their acts to newer but less architecturally pleasing downtown venues. The Assembly House was eventually dismantled, its top and great hall cut away, and its body split into two buildings. The Jefferson and Franklin function halls, along with Congress Hall and Peirce Hall, plus two converted churches, the Cameneum and the Temple, would have to suffice until the Music Hall arrived. ❧

ABOVE: *Portsmouth's vibrant maritime economy crashed soon after 1800 due to a series of downtown fires and Thomas Jefferson's Embargo Act of 1807. Intended as a warning to the British to keep their hands off American merchant ships and to stop impressing American sailors, the law backfired, cutting Atlantic seaports like Portsmouth off from a lucrative international trade. In this 1812 political cartoon the turtle "Ograbme" is "Embargo" spelled backwards. (WIK)*

CHAPTER 2

Come to the Temple
The American Lyceum Movement hits town

The sharp crack of artillery fire echoed across open fields and bells clanged in salute as President James Monroe, escorted by the local cavalry and private citizens in carriages, crossed the town line from Greenland to Portsmouth on Saturday, July 12, 1817. Hundreds of local boys dressed in neat uniforms lined both sides of Middle Street leading to the city center. As the presidential entourage approached Market Square, a military band burst into song amid a throng of spectators, some of whom had been on hand during the last presidential visit in 1789.

But this was not the bustling seaport that had impressed George Washington during his four-day tour almost three decades earlier. In the intervening years Portsmouth had been flattened by fire and drained by the War of 1812, which, despite its name, had dragged on until 1815. The boom days were over and the city would never regain its shipping status as a world trade center. Which is why, when the prominent attorney Jeremiah Mason welcomed President Monroe, his speech sounded more like a cry for help. The city was "now suffering under a temporary depression," Mason told Monroe. But the citizens of the devastated port city had "entire confidence," Mason added, that the fifth American president would use his newfound clout to provide "all the protection and support" the city craved.

Like Washington before him, wishing to offend no one, Monroe was careful to attend multiple church services. The last

ABOVE: *Following three downtown fires, a crushing maritime trade embargo, and an extended war with Britain, Portsmouth was in dire economic straits when James Monroe, fifth President of the United States, visited in 1817. (WHH/WIK)*

OPPOSITE: *No image of the Temple on Chestnut Street, site of the Music Hall, has yet been found. This view shows the Methodist Church, later the Salvation Army building on Pleasant Street, now privately owned. The alley to the right is Porter Street, formerly Prison Lane. Only the bell tower of the Temple is visible in the distance. Once home to the Portsmouth Lyceum, the Temple burned in 1876. Collection of Tom Hardiman. (ATH)*

of the "cocked hat" presidents, again like Washington, Monroe met with his fellow revolutionary, John Langdon, at his Pleasant Street mansion. While Washington had attended a gala ball with "many handsome ladies," Monroe was treated to a more subdued concert by the town's Social Harmonic Society. He may have preferred the livelier theatrical performance of *Abaellino, the Great Bandit*, a popular melodrama that was being staged across town.

Although the Music Hall would not be built for another sixty years, we can trace its lineage to a sense of national unity that flourished during Monroe's two-term presidency. His symbolic 1817 tour of New England prior to taking office kicked off what historians call "The Era of Good Feelings," a healing postwar period marked by optimism. Eventually racial and regional problems would tear the nation in half. But for a few relatively calm years, Americans, north and south, became interested in gaining useful knowledge, in self-improvement, and in discovering what united rather than divided them. A system of public lectures known as the "lyceum movement" flourished in towns across Europe and the United States. In Portsmouth these increasingly entertaining lectures paved the way for the city's first full-time and only surviving historic theater.

Great again?

The boisterous and very public visit by President Monroe coincides with the quiet and private creation of the Portsmouth Athenaeum in 1817. Derived from the name Athena, the Greek goddess of wisdom, athenaeums were centers of learning, culture, and discussion popular in the early 1800s. Wealthy and influential members or "proprietors" pooled their resources to purchase books and periodicals in what was part library, part English-style coffee house, and part chamber of commerce. Unlike earlier social libraries, athenaeums pledged to focus on "useful" books that would aid personal and professional self-improvement. Only sixteen out of hundreds of American athenaeums survive today, many in port cities like Newport and Providence, Rhode Island,

ABOVE: *The Portsmouth Athenaeum, established in 1817, was a membership library as well as the social, business, political, and cultural hub of local merchants, ministers, and maritime men. The term is derived from Athena, the Greek goddess of wisdom and the classical temple of the arts and sciences named to honor her. (MIS)*

OPPOSITE: *Only sixteen out of hundreds of athenaeum organizations have survived in the United States. The Portsmouth Athenaeum, located in Market Square, maintains a library of over 40,000 volumes and an archive of manuscripts, photographs, objects, and ephemera relating to local history. It also sponsors exhibitions, concerts, lectures, and other educational and cultural programs. (ATH)*

in Boston and Salem, Massachusetts, and in Portsmouth, New Hampshire.

By 1823 the Portsmouth Athenaeum was located in a handsome brick Federal-style building at the heart of the city's Market Square. Its first floor reading room, still active today, became the cultural, intellectual, and economic hub of the city. It was, initially, a private men's club frequented by clergymen, merchants, lawyers, printers, ship owners, and ship captains. Here information was shared, deals were made, and ideas were hatched. One of those ideas would eventually turn Portsmouth from a faded maritime shipping center into a top-rated destination for heritage tourism. The slow transformation, however, would take almost two centuries.

What the depressed Portsmouth citizens needed in 1823 — those who had not fled to distant and more prosperous cities — was a booster shot filled with hope and self-respect. Struggling to reinvigorate New Hampshire's only seaport, the wealthy and influential men of Portsmouth threw a party. Three years earlier Plymouth, Massachusetts, had cleverly branded the 1620 arrival

BELOW: (left) This 1867 monumental canopy housed the legendary Plymouth Rock in Massachusetts until it was replaced in 1920. (WIK)

(right) Famed orator and politician Daniel Webster (1782-1852) cut his teeth as a young lawyer in Portsmouth before moving on in 1813 to serve as a U.S. Congressman from Massachusetts. (HMA/WIK)

of the *Mayflower* as the founding site of New England, and by extension, the entire United States. The myth of a nation founded on religious freedom by pious Pilgrims was born at Plymouth on December 21, 1820, at a celebration dubbed Forefathers Day.

In May of 1823, spearheaded by Athenaeum members, Portsmouth held a copycat bicentennial bash, based on the city's founding date of 1623. It was a stretch. Technically, New Hampshire's first European settlers had set up a fishing outpost in April 1623 at what is now the town of Rye. The settlement had lasted only four years. But that inconspicuous event was excuse

BELOW: *Once the key destination for Portsmouth entertainments, the Assembly House was supplanted early in the nineteenth century by the old Franklin Hall on Congress Street and other later venues. This structure, seen here around 1860, was later replaced by the expansive Franklin Block. (ATH)*

enough for Portsmouth to launch a day of parades, speeches, and feasting, topped with a "superb ball" that evening.

That night hundreds of well-dressed ladies and gentlemen gathered at Franklin Hall on Congress Street, site of the Franklin Block today. The highlight of the event was a unique exhibit of about thirty portraits collected from local families who flourished before the Revolution. Portraits of the Wentworths, Sherburnes, Jaffreys, Warners, Havens, Sparhawks, and Atkinsons lined the walls. One portrait, painted in 1623, had been shipped in by family descendants. Another ancestral portrait had been painted in Scotland in 1555. Over the next few days the public was allowed to gaze for the first time at the aristocratic families that had once ruled the port. With the city's financial future in jeopardy, Portsmouth's past appeared idyllic, if only for a few privileged families. The burning question, as the nation approached its half-century mark, was how to make Portsmouth great again.

BELOW: *The Portsmouth Lyceum, like thousands of lecture groups across the country, took its name from the school of the Greek philosopher Aristotle dating to 335 B.C. Italian artist Raphael imagined the famed School of Athens in this 1509 painting featuring Socrates, Aristotle, Ptolemy, Plato, Pythagoras, and Alexander the Great. (WIK)*

Get smart

Nothing announced the end of the old revolutionary way of life better than the simultaneous death of two former presidents. John Adams and Thomas Jefferson both passed away on July 4, 1826, precisely half a century after the adoption of the Declaration of Independence. A new generation of Americans was drawn to a very different type of rebellion, spurred forward by advances in science and mechanics. The Industrial Revolution would transform life in New England, especially in agriculture, in textile manufacturing, and in building railways. While most colleges continued to offer a "classical" education steeped in Latin and Greek, American workers and their employers wanted more practical instruction. The past, as glorious as it may have been for their elders, was past. The new generation wanted to grow up, get smarter, and make money.

In 1826 an itinerant teacher and farmer named Josiah Holbrook gave a series of lectures on science, art, literature, and politics in Millbury, Massachusetts. His adult students, mostly mechanics and other farmers, were hungry for "useful knowledge," Holbrook wrote. Borrowing from the ancient Greek schooling system of Aristotle, Holbrook called his cluster of lectures a "lyceum." The name and the concept quickly caught on. While the athenaeum movement provided a center for edification in the arts and sciences to members of a private men's club, the lyceum movement offered the same benefits to the public at large.

Holbrook promoted his American Lyceum Society concept from town to town, urging schools to offer extracurricular lectures, discussions, and demonstrations, and to collect books, minerals, plants, and other items as aids to education. He advocated for advanced teacher training, for compiling town histories, and especially for including women equally in all lyceums. Holbrook advocated for expanded town libraries and for inexpensive courses (from fifty cents to two dollars per cycle of lectures). The speakers must also be entertaining, he explained, so that their topics "be brought within the comprehension of the most untutored mind."

Josiah Holbrook's Lyceum Society also had a strong moral component. Good lecture topics, he reported, led to more

ABOVE: *New England farmer and teacher Josiah Holbrook (1788-1854) launched the American Lyceum Society that brought grassroots educational lectures to men and women throughout the expanding nation. (MIS)*

elevated and stimulating conversation within a community. This uplifting talk would then replace frivolous conversation, gossip, and petty scandal. A more enlightened population could better appreciate "the works and law of their Creator" and spread "moral prosperity" across the country. Shaping the character of the "rising generation" was the surest way to mold the destiny of the United States, he wrote.

Within a year of Holbrook's initial lecture series, a hundred town lyceums sprang up nearby. By 1833 when Portsmouth officially joined the movement there were 3,000 locations in towns across America. In his seminal study, *The American Lyceum: Town Meeting of the Mind*, the eminent scholar Carl Bode mildly chastised Portsmouth for its late adoption of the lyceum concept. But there's more to that story.

The *NH Farmer's Almanac* for 1827 lists three literary and scientific societies operating in Portsmouth by 1826. The Portsmouth Athenaeum, as we know, had formed a decade earlier. There was also a debate and lecture group known as the

Portsmouth Forensic Club. Third on the list, curiously, was the Portsmouth Lyceum, formed the very same year that Holbrook conducted his first lyceum in Massachusetts.

Details are sketchy, but a rare document archived at the NH Historical Society sheds light on the mystery. The original Portsmouth Lyceum, this fragile artifact proves, was an experimental, all-female private school organized by a man with the colorful name of Rev. Orange Clark. A Canadian-born preacher, Clark drifted in and out of Portsmouth in the early 1800s. He briefly rented rooms at Portsmouth Academy, the handsome brick building now home to Discover Portsmouth on Middle Street. His school offered a challenging five-year course of study. Girls aged eleven and up studied subjects from mathematics, logic, and Latin to astronomy, rhetoric, and ecclesiastical history.

Three years later, however, Orange Clark and his Portsmouth Lyceum were gone. He later popped up in Concord, Massachusetts, where he lectured to teachers on the biblical acceptance of physically punishing wayward boys. ("Thou shalt beat him with the rod, and shalt deliver his soul from hell." *Proverbs 23.*) The itinerant teacher made it all the way to San Francisco, then returned to Canada where he died.

Rev. Clark apparently abandoned his version of an all-female lyceum when he could find no further funding. It is not clear why it took locals five more years to reboot the official Portsmouth Lyceum, but the two institutions are linked. We know because, on the evening of October 26, 1827, Rev. Charles Burroughs, rector of St. John's Episcopal Church, delivered a lecture to the "female school" run by Orange Clark. Burroughs' "Address on Female Education" was so well received that the women in the class requested a published copy. It was Rev. Charles Burroughs, then president of the Portsmouth Athenaeum, with two other prominent men, who established the true Portsmouth Lyceum a few years later in 1833. Their bold signatures can be seen in the surviving hand-written, leather-bound records in the Athenaeum archive.

The entire history of women, Burroughs told his young female audience in 1827, had been "marked with degradation and oppression" due mostly to the "ignorance, overbearing pride, and licentiousness" of men. But those days were over,

ABOVE: *Rev. Charles Burroughs (1787-1868) was rector of St. John's Episcopal Church, president of the Portsmouth Athenaeum, and a key figure in the early Portsmouth Lyceum. (ATH)*

ABOVE: *The early nineteenth-century concept of "republican motherhood" encouraged the education of women primarily so they could pass on patriotic American ideals to their children, especially their sons. The painting is by James Peale. (WIK)*

Burroughs promised the students. America was entering an age of enlightenment, he said, "when the spirit of improvement with its magical wand is giving a transforming touch to everything around us." But Burroughs' lecture, delivered a century before American women gained the right to vote, was no feminist manifesto. An educated woman, he explained, should not consider becoming a professor, or preacher, or politician. Instead, women should apply their newfound knowledge to use in the home. A liberal education, Burroughs said, offered women the freedom to raise wiser children, especially boys, and to enhance their role as friend and companion to their future husbands. Smarter women, Burroughs implied, might also have a better chance of getting into heaven. This viewpoint, popular at the time and now known as "republican motherhood," encouraged the education of women primarily so they could pass on the civic and moral values of their husbands.

The Cameneum

The official Portsmouth Lyceum, the public lecture series inspired by Josiah Holbrook, opened its doors at 6 p.m. on a Tuesday in November 1833. It was an instant success. For its first twenty years, before moving to the future site of the Music Hall, the lyceum found a home two blocks away in an early theater all but forgotten by history. Erected as a Universalist Church in 1784, the building stood on Vaughan Street (now Vaughan Mall) at what is currently Worth Parking Lot. A young lawyer named Daniel Webster once lived next door. The church then served local Methodists for twenty years until it was sold in 1828.

Remodeled by investors, the downtown structure then became an intimate 400-seat theater, ideal for the experimental new lyceum lecture series. Response was so great that those wishing to attend courses were required to list their names on a "subscription paper" posted at Mr. John W. Abbott's store. Those lucky enough to obtain tickets were treated to a half-hour concert by the ever-present Portsmouth Cornet Band, followed at 7 p.m. by a lecture on geology. Rev. Charles Burroughs, it was announced, would focus the second lecture on the art of sculpture.

At first, lyceum speakers were selected from the best and brightest men of the community. Andrew Halliburton, for example, an aging local bank teller and customs collector, was quickly thrust onto a small stage lit by smoky gas lanterns. Halliburton, who addressed the composition and importance of clean air, had long been considered "one of the most agreeable and useful lecturers we have among us." The following week Charles Brewster, the highly respected editor of the *Portsmouth Journal*,

ABOVE: Portsmouth Journal *editor Charles W. Brewster (1802-1869) (top) and anti-war activist William Ladd (1778-1841) (bottom) were among the early speakers at the Portsmouth Lyceum. (JDR/WIK)*

delivered a lecture on the printing process, which he then published for sale as a pamphlet. Lyceum co-founder Dr. Charles Cheever packed the house as he explained how the "science" of phrenology could measure any man's intelligence and assess his character by the shape of his skull. (The newspaper jokingly called this "bumpology.") William Ladd, a ship captain and leader of the peace movement in America, explained why war, all war, was against the teachings of the Gospel. Other topics in the cycle included: zoology, painting, how the mind works, how blood circulates, money, the U.S. Constitution, Dante's *Divine Comedy,* horticulture, and the stellar characters of George Washington and Benjamin Franklin.

The *Portsmouth Journal* rejoiced in the creation of the new lecture series, but the editor regretted that very few men below the age of twenty-one, the targeted lyceum audience, were attending "the feast of reason." While a rare few feared that educating common men made them disobedient to the law, it was generally accepted that wiser young men made better citizens. A few in attendance complained to the editor about uncomfortable backless wooden seats. The biggest problem, however, came from the stylish ladies who outnumbered men by two-to-one. In the fashion of the day, many women wore large straw hats or "leghorns" that blocked almost everyone's view of the speaker.

"It is by no means becoming to the beautiful face," a reader protested in the *Portsmouth Journal*, "[and] only helps to conceal . . . I trust the bonnet will be hereafter banished from the lecture-room, and that ladies hereafter will wear hoods which they can take off immediately after they are seated." The letter was signed by "A Looker-on" and bonnets were soon banned during lyceum lectures.

As the concept of low-cost public lectures caught on in Portsmouth and as audiences grew, more rules followed. Announcing the cycle of topics for 1835, the *Portsmouth Journal* listed new lyceum regulations including:

- All talking, whispering, and unnecessary walking about during the delivery of the lecture are expressly prohibited.
- In all lectures sentiments calculated to give offense on religion or politics are to be avoided.

ABOVE: *Among the city's most enduring images is the arch. Usually made of greenery and wood, arches were constructed over streets leading to Market Square as a welcoming sign to visitors. The Jubilee Arch seen here was among the decorations in an 1853 celebration. (ATH)*

- It is expressly understood that no member's ticket can be transferred except in the family of the member, and that it will admit one gentleman and two ladies.
- No gentlemen shall deliver any lecture before the lyceum unless his subject be known and approved by the board of directors.

Growing pains were inevitable as the weekly lyceum talks became the must-see event in a world without movies, radio, recorded music, television, the internet, or even photography. The "explosion of American speech" in the coming decades, according to one historian, was distinctly democratic. The lyceum movement combined the familiar elements of church, school, town meeting, and the theater into a single social gathering.

The little theater on Vaughan Street was also ideal for performances. The city was awash with well-organized musical groups from the Social Harmonic Society to the Portsmouth Handel Society. "A singing mania has been very prevalent here this winter," one young Portsmouth woman wrote to a friend.

In 1839 the best singers of the many churches banded together to form the Portsmouth Sacred Music Society. Following a hugely successful concert they raised funds and purchased the

ABOVE: It was publisher James T. Fields, born in Portsmouth, who persuaded British superstar, Charles Dickens, (1812-1870) to come to the United States in 1867. In a whirlwind five-month tour, Dickens gave dramatic readings of his popular novels, including A Christmas Carol. *The sold-out tour was a critical and financial triumph. (CDM/WIK)*

building that would be renamed "The Cameneum." Then they hired a local company to build and install the biggest pipe organ the city had ever seen or heard. Its 600 pipes ranged in height from three-quarters of an inch to seventeen feet tall. The Society also enlarged the stage and increased the audience size to 500, plus one hundred seats in the upper gallery.

It was at the dedication in the summer of 1840 that Rev. Charles Burroughs, a classical scholar, christened the hall with its new name. He called it "The Cameneum," an invented Greek-sounding word he translated as "Home of the Arts and Muses." It was a terrible name, but it was a great little hall with the best acoustics, and it was frequently the only show in town.

For the next dozen years, the Portsmouth Lyceum renewed its contract with various owners of the Cameneum. President Franklin Pierce, a New Hampshire native, attended a concert there, while famed New England writers Oliver Wendell Holmes and Nathaniel Hawthorne were speakers. In 1852, around the time he lectured in Portsmouth and vacationed at the Isles of Shoals, Hawthorne parodied the lyceum practice. In his novel, *The Blithedale Romance*, his main character visits a small Massachusetts town.

"The scene was one of those lyceum halls," Hawthorne wrote, "of which almost every village has now its own, dedicated to that sober and pallid, or rather drab-colored mode of winter-evening entertainment — the lecture." But by the mid-nineteenth

century, Hawthorne noted in his novel, dry didactic lectures were increasingly interspersed with light entertainment. While true vaudeville was still a few decades away, lyceum venues were beginning to liven things up with visiting ventriloquists, magicians, and black singers, or white singers in blackface. Lecturers enhanced their educational talks with real skeletons, dioramas, moving panoramas, and wax figures.

The Cameneum went through a final facelift in the early 1850s at the hands of a talented local teacher, marine painter, floral designer, poet, and organist named Thomas P. Moses. It was Moses who introduced an art gallery space, reduced the size of the Cameneum stage, and expanded seating to fit 600. Moses removed an annoying low-hanging chandelier and added brilliant footlights, fresh scenery, and a new drop curtain. The inner ceiling was painted to represent the sky with the sun, moon, stars, and comets. The art gallery featured scenes of Switzerland, Paris, and Italy.

A sometimes sulking, often sickly, frequently explosive, and deeply sensitive character, Thomas Moses may have been the wrong man to turn a profit for the endangered theater. But he dutifully promoted the Cameneum as "the most convenient and beautiful concert and lecture rooms to be found anywhere. Also good for tea parties and fairs and an acting company would find it a great home. It is the place that everybody likes."

Apparently not everyone liked the Cameneum. In the spring of 1853 a group of rude boys were pitched out of the theater. They exacted revenge by destroying the sign promoting an upcoming show. Then "a squad of young rowdies" caused a disturbance during Mr. Thompson's Ethiopian concert. Local law enforcement needed to "show more energy," one reporter suggested. "Let the police take from these meetings a few of the ringleaders, and put them in the Watch House; we should soon see a difference in the conduct of the young men," he wrote.

By this time trains routinely steamed in and out of the city, allowing culture devotees to travel greater distances to view shows in Boston. By 1854, with his artistic prospects dwindling in Portsmouth, even Thomas Moses chose to abandon his beloved hometown for the promise of the big city. A reporter for the *Portsmouth Chronicle* offered this analysis in 1856:

Theatricals have been at a rather low ebb in Portsmouth for the last twenty-five years. There are many among our citizens, who enjoy dramatic representations, but prefer to visit Boston occasionally, and witness a play effectually put upon the stage, rather than patronize companies such as usually appear among us, here at home. We have not often been favored with a series of really good dramatic representations in this city, and people hesitate to patronize a traveling theater.

The slow demise of the once "cozy delightful little hall" was particularly grim. In 1863, as the Civil War raged, the Cameneum was purchased by Nathan Jones, whose brother Frank Jones, the "ale tycoon," would soon become the city's dominant businessman and an owner of the Music Hall. Nathan Jones intended to build a hotel on the Cameneum site, but settled for a parking lot, livery, and billiard room. Over time his American Stables company expanded into the theater building itself, then used for "the stowage of carriages." In 1883 a fire started in the hayloft of what was then Stoddard's Stable. The flames spread quickly. Thirty sleighs, a number of carriages, forty tons of hay, and twenty-four horses were consumed by the blaze.

ABOVE: *From church to theater to stable to parking lot, the Cameneum on Vaughan Street has been largely forgotten as a venue for performing arts in Portsmouth. (ATH)*

RIGHT: *A rare Civil War-era handbill shows the variety of entertainment at the Temple on Chestnut Street. In addition to a selection from Shakespeare, a fancy dance, and patriotic music, audiences enjoyed a performance of* Our Female American Cousin. *This is not to be confused with the play* Our American Cousin, *the comedy later performed at Ford's Theater on the night of the assassination of Abraham Lincoln. But curiously, the star of the Temple production mentioned on the handbill is Miss Helen Western, who with her sister Lucile Western was apparently a one-time girlfriend of John Wilkes Booth. Hers was one of five photographs of women Booth had in his pocket when he was killed. At the time Booth was reportedly engaged to Lucy Hale of nearby Dover, New Hampshire. From the collection of Kevin LaFond. (KLC)*

AT THE TEMPLE.

TWO NIGHTS MORE!

BENEFIT OF THE
THE BEAUTIFUL STAR, MISS HELEN,
MONDAY EVE'NG, JUNE 17,

On which occasion the performance will commence with William B. English's celebrated Three Act Play of the

FEMALE

American Cousin!

Pamelia, with Song,   Miss Helen,

And Dance her Great Character Dance, "SHIN IN, PITCH IN."

Sir James Hazlette, a nobleman,	Mr. J. McTier	Fitzherbert, lisping, snobbish,	Mr. C. H. Clarke
Nathan Bennett, a sharp, Yankee lawyer,	Mr. Hampton	Biddles,	E. B. Williams
		Sir Charles, a sprig of nobility,	Mr. Dillon
		Capt. Granville, a leaf of nobility,	Mr. R. Smith
Howard, born in England, but inclined	Mr. Davis	Biddy Fagan, a nondescript,	Miss Mason
to Yankeedom,	Miss Gale	Clara,	Miss Hampton
Lady Hazlett,	Miss Boniface	Amelia,	Miss Baker
Lady Lisington,			

After which, Fancy Dance by Miss Boniface.

After which a Grand Display, called the

Defence Of the Union!

Dedicated to the

Second Regiment, New Hampshire Volunteers,

in which Miss Helen will Sing "THE STARS AND STRIPES," with full Chorus by the Company.

The Entertainment will commence with the 3d Act of

OTHELLO.

Othello,   Mr. Boniface.   Iago,   Mr. Davis.

The Entertainment to conclude with

Robert Macaire.

Robert Macaire,	Mr. Boniface	Jaques Strop,	Mr. Hampton
Mr. Germent,	Mr. Williams	Dumo t,	Mr. McTier
Charles,	Davis	Pierre,	Watson
Clementine,	Miss Boniface	Maria,	Miss Gale

Doors open 7 1-2, Performance to commence at 8 o'clock.

Admittance-----25 Cents ; Children 15 Cents.

PARTICULAR NOTICE.

I cannot be responsible for any goods but for the use of the Theatre, unless authorized by my written order.   W. B. ENGLISH.

N. B. *Gazette Press, Daniel Street, Portsmouth.*

Culture club

In the mid-1850s the popular Portsmouth Lyceum needed more seats than the Cameneum could offer and its managers moved it to a larger venue about two blocks away. Besides a ghostly view of the bell tower, we have no photograph of the Temple, the third and final home of the lyceum on Chestnut Street where the Music Hall stands today. Like the Portsmouth Athenaeum, the Portsmouth Lyceum, and the Cameneum, the Temple was named in homage to the enlightened culture of ancient Greece. But it too had begun as a church and had a significant history even before the arrival of the Portsmouth Lyceum.

The church was constructed by the Baptist Society of Portsmouth on the site of the town's colonial prison and almshouse. Elias Smith, the founder of the church, holds a unique

ABOVE: *Scottish inventor Alexander Graham Bell (1847-1922) demonstrates his telephone at the Lyceum Hall in Salem, Massachusetts, in 1877. (MIS)*

place in American religious history. A traveling preacher, Smith was in debt and on the verge of despair when he arrived in Portsmouth in 1802. Considered a radical and an activist, Smith believed that every person had the inalienable right to read the Bible and interpret its meaning. He railed against what he saw as the tyranny of Christian ministers and church dogma. During an era of religious awakening in America, Smith discovered a small but loyal following in Portsmouth and preached at various halls downtown before building his own church on Chestnut Street. His congregation, at first, were mobbed by those who saw the Baptists as a threat to traditional Christian churches.

Smith is best known today for launching the first-ever religious newspaper, published in Portsmouth. His *Herald of Gospel Liberty* explored the essential truths in all religions and was open to writers and readers of all faiths. His church, too, was open to preachers of various sects. Smith bounced in and out of Portsmouth over the years, eventually converting to Unitarian

BELOW: *Like the Cameneum, the Temple began as a house of worship and was slowly adapted to a more theater-like design with a stage instead of altar and arena seating instead of pews. This plan comes from 1845 when the building was operated by the Portsmouth Washingtonian Total Abstinence Society. (MHC)*

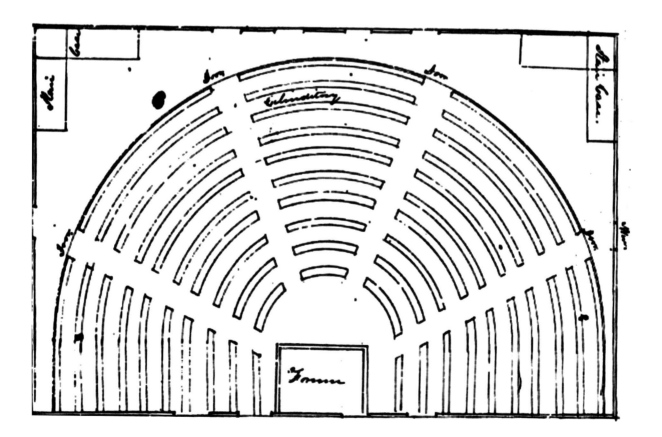

beliefs. The expanding Baptist congregation moved to another location on Pleasant Street. The church was purchased in 1839 by Benjamin Cheever and Joseph M. Edmonds and used initially by the First Christian Society.

In the early 1840s, like the Cameneum just down the street, the building was redesigned and enlarged, making it more attractive, less churchy, and more theater-like. The pews, pulpit, and gallery were removed. The interior was rebuilt in the shape of an amphitheater with an increased seating capacity of 800 to 1,000. Rebranded as the "Temple," the redesigned hall became "an ornament of the town" and a central gathering place.

This proto-theater quickly became a hotspot for proponents of the temperance movement then sweeping the nation. A contemporary writer in the *Christian Journal* made the dubious claim that 5,000 out of 8,000 Portsmouth inhabitants had taken a "pledge of abstinence from all intoxicating liquors" and that places serving alcohol in town had been reduced from 125 to about forty. Referring to the Temple on Chestnut Street, the *Journal* reported:

> There has lately been opened a beautiful and commodious *Temperance Hall*, which I trust will give an impetus to the cause . . . May this Hall be the place where many shall be persuaded to sign the pledge, and become the occasion of drying up many a tear of woe!

By 1847 the Temple was home to the Washington Total Abstinence Society, a group founded by six alcoholics from

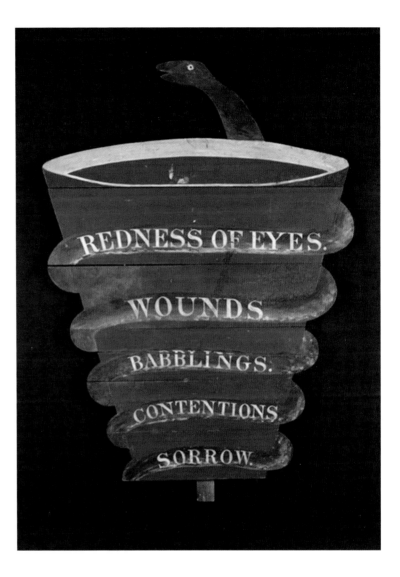

ABOVE: *A temperance signboard painted on wood from New Hampshire depicting a snake encircling a cup, circa 1896. Photo by Franz Nicolay. (SHS/PHS)*

Maryland who campaigned against all spirituous and intoxicating liquors. "Many a man was rescued from a drunkard's grave by their efforts," according to a Portsmouth newspaper. The Washingtonians lasted only one year there, but the Temple flourished. New owners in 1859 and 1867 expanded the number of seats and deepened the stage to accommodate more dramatic shows. The larger size and improved acoustics made the Temple stiff competition for the fading Cameneum.

The Temple began pulling in bigger, more secular acts including the popular Hutchinson Family Singers. This musical farming family from Milford, New Hampshire, sang about temperance, abolition, patriotism, and rural life. Their lively protest songs are often compared to the American folk music revolution of the 1950s and 60s.

Another popular act with a similar name, the Hammon Family gave a "one night only" performance at the Temple early in 1847. An ad in the local newspaper reveals the tricky balance between booking morally uplifting shows that also sold tickets and filled seats. The Hammons were apostate Shakers who had renounced the "Shaking Quaker" religious community in Alfred, Maine. Dressed in Shaker outfits, the group spoke about the Shaker's curious beliefs, including the segregation of male and female members. They sang Shaker songs, and danced the

ABOVE: Temple audiences were fascinated by the singing and dancing of "Shaking Quakers" or Shakers, who combined marching and spinning into their religious services as performed by groups like the Hammon Family. This image comes from a popular lithograph. (MIS)

spectacular "whirling gift," in which a woman spun in circles hundreds of times. The newspaper ad for the Hammons promised that the "entirely new" musical show was refined, but also entertaining, "blending instruction and amusement for the gratification of the grave and gay."

That same newspaper issue offers us a snapshot of New Hampshire's only port city. Alongside a notice for the Hammon Family concert, the "People's Lyceum" announced its next talk about a newly discovered planet named Neptune. The astronomy lecture was illustrated by a series of paintings. Meanwhile, another ad invited Portsmouth residents to visit the nearby studio of J.P. Plumer, an early daguerreotype photographer. Plumer guaranteed his customers miniature lifelike pictures taken "in the highest perfection of the art." The railroad, too, had arrived in Portsmouth, and the tourists were soon on their way. It was during this heady time, with the clouds of war looming, that the Portsmouth Lyceum found its third and final home at the Temple on Chestnut Street.

ABOVE: *The Hutchinson Family Singers of Milford, New Hampshire, were the ideal act in an age of moral entertainment prior to the Civil War. Their songs focused on temperance, abolition, patriotism, and rural life. (MET/ WIK)*

The opinion makers

Just as the Music Hall will provide us with a microcosm of the vaudeville and cinema eras in future chapters, we can follow the American Lyceum movement as it evolved in Portsmouth. True to Josiah Holbrook's vision, it began as a kind of adult education system where the town's most intelligent individuals passed their knowledge to the community at large. But it quickly morphed into a series of random lectures often delivered by outsiders. Portsmouth Lyceum talks bounced among topics from the making of silk to Scottish poetry, the Boston Tea Party, the anatomy of romance, and the causes of insanity.

The lyceum stage became the ideal forum for the rise of many American reform movements prior to the Civil War. Reformers railed against the evils of slavery and alcohol, the dangers of eating meat, the poor treatment of women, the threat of wealthy capitalists, the failures of elite colleges, and the exploitation of American laborers. The most popular performers who sold the most tickets got the best gigs as they travelled within a widening lecture "circuit" from town to town and hall to hall. Public speaking became a lucrative profession for pop stars like naturalist Henry David Thoreau, comedian Artemus Ward, novelist Mark Twain, abolitionist Sojourner Truth, women's rights activist Susan B. Anthony and scores more. Portsmouth-born writers James T. Fields and B.P. Shillaber were among the "Kings of the Platform."

The flowering of Ralph Waldo Emerson, for example, from a Unitarian minister to a rock star of the lectern is an ideal example. His progression from pulpit to podium gave Emerson the chance to expound on topics that fascinated him. In our brief lives, he told his enrapt audience, each person's goal is to cast off outside influences and "know thyself." As his philosophy of "self-reliance" developed, so did his fan base and his lecture fees. Lecturers including Emerson were initially paid $5, about $130 today. The fee rose steadily to $100, $200, even $500, equal to thousands of dollars per show for a modern celebrity speaker.

Standing six-foot-tall, the handsome yet gangly young man looked like a prosperous farmer, according to one contemporary witness. Drawing from his years as a preacher, he projected his voice towards the back of the hall. Emerson trumpeted his message of hope and optimism through independence and nonconformity. What's fascinating about Emerson is that he recorded his ideas in extensive journals, then honed his philosophy in front of an audience, beginning with the Concord Lyceum in his Massachusetts hometown. Emerson then took these lectures, each filling forty handwritten pages, on the road, delivering at least 1,500 talks in his lifetime. Only after shaping his philosophy in front of a live audience, did he finally write and publish them as essays.

"You carry your fortunes in your own hand," Emerson shouted at his audience, hammering his right fist against the lyceum lectern. "You are the universe to yourself." This was heady stuff in the mid-1800s. Those words would later inspire a generation of free-love, back-to-the-earth, mind-expanding young people in the swinging 1960s who adopted Emerson's teachings.

American audiences, increasingly mobile and gainfully employed, now wanted to be entertained, inspired, and challenged. Portsmouth citizens flocked to see the fiery Frederick Douglass, a former slave, when he spoke at the Temple in 1862 on the future of black Americans. That same year twenty-five black sailors took the stage to sing sacred songs and deliver their opinion about the detestable conditions of slavery. But Portsmouth audiences applauded with equal enthusiasm on evenings when white singers, dressed in blackface, performed the same songs in racist minstrel show parodies.

Frederick Buckley, one of the most famous blackface minstrels of his day, gave his final performance at the Portsmouth Temple on June 22, 1864. A member of an English family troupe, Buckley's Serenaders, Frederick was also a composer of popular tunes like "Break It Gently to My Mother," "Lily White," and "Come in and Shut the Door." After holding the crowded Temple audience spellbound with the "sweet strains of Negro music," the thirty-one-year-old white performer returned to Boston and died the same day.

Temple audiences, as if anticipating vaudeville, were eager to see acts like Signor Blitz, a popular English mesmerist, ventriloquist, juggler, and bird wrangler who specialized in catching bullets in midair. And while the Portsmouth Lyceum did its best

ABOVE: *King of the lyceum platform and a leader of the Transcendentalism movement, Ralph Waldo Emerson (1803-1882) refined his theories in over 1,500 lectures. (WIK)*

to stick with the ethical and educational standards espoused by its founders, other lyceum venues were drawn to "low arts" and unvarnished "theatricality."

The Fox sisters, for example, Margaret, Kate, and Leah, became well known mediums, summoning the tapping of spirits from the grave, until their act was revealed as a hoax. (Margaret eventually confessed to loudly cracking her toe joints that echoed mysteriously throughout theaters.) Some educational venues were reduced to unwrapping small mummies, imported from Egypt, to the ghoulish delight of ticket-holders.

In 1873 Portsmouth threw itself another anniversary bash. While the 1823 bicentennial had been a rather somber pity party, designed to rally economically depressed locals, the 250th "Return of the Sons and Daughters" was part nostalgia, part commercial genius. Huge wooden arches draped in greenery welcomed thousands of prodigal visitors back to New Hampshire's only colonial port, faded but still standing.

That summer, with tourist hotels popping up along the seacoast, optimists predicted a post-Civil War revival for the former aristocratic capital. On the Isles of Shoals, a cluster of rocky islands ten miles from Portsmouth, the Appledore Hotel was filled to capacity, as was its newly built neighbor, the Oceanic Hotel on Star Island nearby. Boston area artists and intellectuals were drawn to the island salon of Portsmouth-born poet Celia Thaxter, whose family ran the Appledore. Many of her summer guests were the same superstars — including actor Edwin Booth, social reformer Henry Ward Beecher, musicians Ole Bull and Julius Eichberg, poets Henry Wadsworth Longfellow and John Greenleaf Whittier, essayist William Dean Howells — who had populated the now-waning lyceum stage. Other famous New England speakers often rusticated with artistic friends at New Castle and Little Harbor.

The lyceum idea never really died. The global proliferation of twenty-first-century TED talks, where eloquent, informed

ABOVE: *Born enslaved, abolitionist Frederick Douglass (1818-1895) became an author, statesman, and advisor to Abraham Lincoln. In 1862 Douglass delivered a speech at the Temple in Portsmouth entitled "The Black Man's Future in the Southern States." (MIS)*

speakers deliver "ideas worth sharing," is evidence that Josiah Holbrook was onto something big back in 1826. But by the end of the nineteenth century, the speakers were demanding untenable fees. The market for morally uplifting "useful knowledge" was moving away from the stage and back to the pulpit. And in 1874, an adult education summer assembly of popular speakers, entertainers, musicians, and teachers known as a "Chautauqua" began in New York and would soon replace the lyceum.

Journalist Edward Payson Powell, looking back on the lyceum phenomenon in 1895, saw no reason to mourn. "Forms of education are constantly changing and the American temperament has plasticity to adapt itself," he wrote. Thanks to the lyceum, Powell explained, literary, scientific, and artistic societies were flourishing across the country. Schools were improving and public libraries expanding.

"The lyceum had run its course," the journalist wrote with overweening praise, "but it killed slavery; it broke the power of superstitious ideology; it made women free; it created a universal demand for higher culture . . . I do not believe New England ever affected the world more positively and aggressively than from the platform."

The Portsmouth Lyceum, like so much of the city's history, disappeared in flames. It expired in the night when the Temple caught fire on Christmas Eve in 1876. 🙖

ABOVE: *Many of the speakers best known to lyceum audiences were also guests at the summer salon of Portsmouth-born poet and artist Celia Laighton Thaxter (1835-1894) at the Appledore Hotel on the Isles of Shoals. (JDR)*

CHAPTER 3

The Theater Biz

The Peirce family builds a Music Hall

ABOVE: *The hand and torch of the Statue of Liberty on display at the Centennial Exposition in Philadelphia. This 1876 world's fair attracted ten million visitors. (LOC)*

OPPOSITE: *Portsmouth's Peirce family created the Music Hall in 1878 and sold it in 1899. Here family members dress up as their ancestors for the city's Tercentennial Celebration in 1923. They are posed on the front steps of the Peirce Mansion in Haymarket Square. (ATH)*

The Christmas fire that claimed the Temple on Chestnut Street started below the stage on a snowy evening and quickly spread. The flames were both devastating and merciful. Hundreds of members of the Reform Club had planned to pack the wooden theater that very evening for an anti-alcohol holiday rally. It was a Temple custom that, when every seat had been taken, boards were placed across the aisle, turning the only means of escape into temporary bleachers for the overflow audience. Had the fire started an hour later, the *Portsmouth Herald* theorized, "a terrible catastrophe might have resulted . . . It would have been well nigh impossible for many to escape, if any."

The 1876 fire was the final surprise in what had been a surprising year. Having survived its first hundred years and a savage civil war, the United States was moving into an era of unprecedented change and renewal. Ten million visitors attending the Centennial Exhibition in Philadelphia saw a life-altering array of new inventions, including the first telephone, typewriter, dishwasher, carpet sweeper, and sewing machine. A fifty-foot-tall steam engine throbbed inside an enormous exhibition hall. The towering right arm and torch of what would become the Statue of Liberty was on display. Thomas Edison, introducing the first mimeograph machine, was on the verge of unveiling the phonograph and the incandescent bulb. Things would never be the same.

The nation's hundredth birthday was also a time to look backwards. Indeed, it was the intoxicating and often frightening rise of Victorian technology that sparked the "Colonial Revival" in American architecture and popular culture. The headlong rush towards the future was matched by an aching nostalgia for the past. One exhibition at the Philadelphia Centennial offered a reconstructed New England farmhouse. Inside visitors saw a "colonial kitchen," with its large comforting hearth where women wearing pre-revolutionary costumes happily worked their spinning wheel, loom, and butter churn. This fascination with the olden days, both nostalgic and patriotic, spread widely in the coming decades. The renewed passion for the past was especially popular in a city like Portsmouth, already known for its once grand, but deteriorating, Georgian mansions. The Colonial Revival movement romanticized the past, while conveniently

blotting out the cruel realities of slavery, disease, inequality, poverty, hardship, and war.

This rose-colored view of history matched the branding campaign that Portsmouth had been using to draw visitors to its blockbuster homecoming celebrations in 1823, 1853, and 1873. During those fifty years, the nation watched thirteen presidents come and go, suffered the loss of 620,000 Civil War soldiers, and was traumatized by the assassination of "The Great Emancipator," Abraham Lincoln. Compared to the recent war-torn past and the machine-dominated future, the Colonial Era began to symbolize all things safe, simple, and pure.

Portsmouth, meanwhile, had begun a slow but erratic economic recovery. The Portsmouth Naval Shipyard, located across the Piscataqua River in Kittery, had become a key ship-building center in a time of war. But with the Civil War over, scarcely two dozen employees remained on the shipyard payroll in 1877. Portsmouth's biggest business was now beer. The city's only tycoon, Frank Jones, was aggressively expanding one of the largest breweries in the nation. Profits from Frank Jones Ale was

ABOVE: *The USS* Kearsarge, *launched at Portsmouth Naval Shipyard in 1861, is best known for its defeat of the Confederate raider USS* Alabama *during the Civil War. Powered by sail and steam, the sloop of war was a source of immense pride locally. The Peirce family named their Kearsarge House, adjacent to the Music Hall, in its honor. (WIK)*

being funneled into the acquisition of hotels, banks, utilities, insurance companies, and soon — into the Music Hall. But first, someone had to build it.

The Peirce family

With the Cameneum converted to a stable and the Temple reduced to ashes, Portsmouth entered 1877 without a downtown theater. Investing in the burgeoning live entertainment business was a surprising step for the wealthy, conservative Peirce family. Two Peirce sisters, Anna and Sarah, with their brother William, owned the brick Kearsarge House at the corner of Congress and Chestnut streets directly adjoining the burned-out Temple lot. The sudden loss of hundreds of Portsmouth Lyceum patrons passing the doors of their hotel may have inspired the Peirce family to construct a new public entertainment hall.

Even a cursory climb up the Peirce family tree is dizzying (not to mention the "Pierce" and "Pearce" connections). Successful in love, war, and business, they displayed a near genetic ability to turn a profit — from fishing to farming to finance and more. Their patriarch, Daniel Peirce, was a blacksmith from Suffolk, England, who arrived at Newbury, Massachusetts, in 1634. His progeny were soon prominent in Newbury, in Kittery, and in Portsmouth, where they married into the most influential and wealthy colonial families in town. Their genealogy leads us to Col. Joshua Winslow Peirce, a man, according to a family biographer, of great intelligence, vigorous constitution, strict habits, unblemished character, and strong prejudices. He had "a somewhat cold exterior," his biographer noted. Peirce was also a man of "large possessions" when he died in 1874, just two years before the demise of the Temple.

Col. Joshua Peirce was Portsmouth-born and bred like his wife Emily, who was descended from the ancient Sheafe and Wentworth lines. Although scarcely mentioned in her husband's biography, Emily Peirce bore twelve children before her death in 1871. Only half of those children were alive when work on the Music Hall began in 1877. It seems beyond coincidence that all of Col. Peirce's sons chose to live elsewhere, as far away as Texas

ABOVE: *Exquisite spiral stairway of the 1799 John Peirce mansion. The curved settee at the base of the stairs is now at the Winterthur Museum in Delaware. (SBM)*

OPPOSITE: *The circa-1799 Peirce family mansion on Court Street now owned by the Middle Street Baptist Church. (PHS/ATH)*

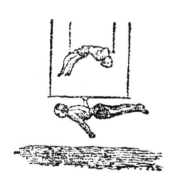

and Wisconsin, and settled back in the Portsmouth area only after their father's death. All three unmarried sons — William, Robert, and Joseph — were wed when the Music Hall project was underway or soon after. Sister Sarah, then in her fifties, also married for the first time the year the Music Hall opened in 1878.

We may never know precisely why the Peirce siblings joined forces to build Portsmouth's grand new house of entertainment. Perhaps, with new theaters rising across the country, they saw a clever way to invest their newly inherited wealth. Perhaps the prodigal sons felt a civic responsibility to their ancestral home-town. Or maybe the kids just wanted to have fun. Whatever their reason, it is a safe bet that the very proper, thrifty, and pious Col. Joshua Peirce would have disapproved.

The Peirce name is spread throughout the city, even today, from Peirce Island, site of the commercial fishing pier and public swimming pool, to the Peirce Commercial Block in Market Square and the 1799 John Peirce mansion on Court Street. Four of the Peirce siblings were living at the mansion in 1877. There was also a Peirce family home on Congress Street, a large working farm in the neighboring town of Greenland, plus rental properties on the north and south ends of town.

The local newspapers made no mention of the lost Temple in the early months of 1877. Lectures and concerts continued in local churches and at smaller downtown venues including Congress Hall, Mechanics Hall, and Franklin Hall. The old Temple and the Portsmouth Lyceum were missed, but not terribly. Life moved on. Snowfall was heavy that winter, the newspaper commented, and horse-drawn sleighs were all the rage. Men in fashionable blue-tinted glasses escorted women sporting the new "raven" hairstyle.

In late March, as patches of green began peeking through the snow, Mrs. Anne R. Peirce Burroughs died. The wealthy widow of the late Rev. Charles Burroughs, the co-founder of the Portsmouth Lyceum, was also the aunt of the six Peirce siblings. "By her death," the *Portsmouth Journal* noted, "the poor lose a kind friend, and every good cause a local helper." Whether Aunt Anne's passing, or her philanthropy, or Rev. Burrough's lyceum lectures at the Temple influenced the decision to build a theater is unclear.

It was around this time that Robert Cutts Peirce, the youngest of the Peirce clan, was appointed treasurer of the newly-formed Piscataqua Savings Bank, today the city's oldest financial institution. At thirty-seven, the former Navy paymaster was suddenly a powerful financial figure in town. He was engaged, not surprisingly, to the daughter of the president of the same bank, the Hon. W.H.Y. Hackett, whom we will hear from very soon. William Augustus Peirce, the second-youngest son at forty-one, was the official owner of the Kearsarge Hotel and was soon to become a driving force in the theater project. Previously a sheep farmer in Texas, William had moved back to the Peirce farm in nearby Greenland after his father's death. William, too, would be married within a year.

LEFT: *Nellie Newell, the daughter of prolific Portsmouth photographer Lafayette V. Newell, strikes a pose with her banjo. When this photo was taken in 1890 the Portsmouth City Directory listed ten music teachers. (SBM)*

OPPOSITE: *Following the Civil War theaters had to compete with bigger and better touring circuses. These images are drawn from a newspaper ad for the Joe Pentland Circus that visited Portsmouth in the 1850s. This early big top show featured tumblers, vaulters, leapers, amateur equestrians, dancers, drummers, and "Triumphs of the Trampoline." The event was preceded by a parade through town with ponies and trained animals. It concluded with a "laughable pantomimic spectacle." (JDR)*

Nothing but the best

Plans for the theater venture were closely held through the winter. Word first reached the media on April 11, 1877 with a revealing tidbit in the *Portsmouth Journal*, a newspaper to which Mr. Hackett was a frequent contributor.

> Arrangements are in progress to build a fine amusement hall, by a stock company, on the site of the Temple which was recently burned. A goodly number of shares at one hundred dollars each have already been subscribed for, and the project is so far advanced that plans for the new temple are being drawn, and estimates making of the cost.

ABOVE: *A crowd gathers to listen to two young street buskers playing violins as their "gypsy" father with his harp looks on. The 1880s picture was taken from the second-floor window of Lafayette Newell's photography studio looking out onto Market Square. (SBM)*

Upon discovering that the heirs of Col. J.W. Peirce were behind the project, the *Journal* gushed its approval. The family's reputation guaranteed "there will be nothing cheap or imperfect in the new building." Learning from mistakes made on previous public halls, the Peirce theater promised to be fireproof, comfortable, acoustically perfect, and filled with "pure atmosphere," that is, breathable air.

Except for those with deep pockets, this was the wrong year for bold new ventures. According to the *Portsmouth City Directory*, 1877 was marked by an "unparalleled depression of business," the continuing fallout from the Financial Panic of 1873. An unprecedented 18,000 firms had failed in the previous two years nationwide. The Portsmouth Naval Shipyard, the city's economic engine during the Civil War, had been scaled down to a handful of workers. The newspaper reported an alarming rise in opium use, while the increasingly poor neighborhood along Water Street (now Prescott Park) was developing into a "red light district" of saloons and bordellos. Young boys were brazenly panhandling in Market Square, and census workers reported visiting homes where whole families had not eaten for days.

In the same month that the *Journal* announced plans for a new theater, editor Lewis Brewster also drew attention to these troubling social issues. "There is more actual suffering from want in this city at the present time, than has been known for months," he wrote in April. This was the year the Odd Fellows, a fraternal charitable organization chose to build their sturdy brick building just a block away on Congress Street, even as they were besieged by requests from the city's poor. And 1877 saw the formation of the Chase House, originally a respite for Portsmouth's orphaned children, that has evolved into a modern safe haven for at-risk youth.

Amid hard times the Peirce project forged ahead with remarkable speed and efficiency. The family hired William Allyn Ashe, a young draftsman at the Portsmouth Naval Shipyard, to design their theater. Originally from Boston, Ashe had arrived at Portsmouth a decade earlier, married a local woman, started a family, and moved into one of the neighborhoods springing up around the city center. With work stalled at the shipyard and the tragic loss of his first child, William Ashe now found himself

ABOVE: *Portrait of Robert Peirce from around 1875, one of the Peirce family siblings who invested in the creation of the Music Hall. (ATH)*

managing the most important construction job in town. He was about to build, according to one contemporary architect, "the premier center for public performances and entertainment on the New Hampshire coast." His design called for a seating capacity of 1,214 with modern central steam heating and gas lighting. Ashe proposed a stage equipped with traps, a bridge, the latest machinery for changing scenery, plus an orchestra pit.

By the first week of June construction was underway. Late in July the *Boston Daily Globe* reported that "the contract for building the stage of the new opera house at Portsmouth, New Hampshire, has been awarded to Frederick Weld & Co., the well-known scenery and stage builders of this city." Weld first appeared in Boston directories as a carpenter, but later described himself as a "theatrical builder." Advertising in the *Harvard Advocate*, Weld offered scenery for "dramatic representations" available for rent or "painted to order."

Despite a dearth of news about the new hall, Portsmouth was watching. According to banker, lawyer, and politician William Henry Young Hackett, the whole town followed the construction of the Music Hall "as the expected owners of an embryo ship

BELOW: *Originally built by the Campbell family of New Castle in 1874, the Wentworth Hotel was greatly expanded and widely promoted by its second owner, Frank Jones, who also owned the Rockingham Hotel adjacent to the new Music Hall. Jones would later do the same for the Music Hall. (ATH)*

watch the laying of the keel and the rising of the frame." Even the influential W.H.Y. Hackett, whose daughter was engaged to Robert Peirce, seemed to be on the outside looking in. "Some of us . . . would, from time to time, have given our opinion if the proprietors had given us an opportunity to form one," Hackett later joked. But the bold "NO ADMITTANCE" signs posted on the brick exterior meant business — and few details leaked out as construction continued.

The summer newspapers of 1877 were filled, instead, with gossip about the lively seaside tourist trade. Visitors from distant cities traveled aboard an expanding network of trains, trolleys, and ferries to rusticate at Boar's Head on Hampton Beach, or at the exclusive Wentworth Hotel in New Castle. The Farragut in Rye boasted the addition of its first telephone, connecting the hotel office with the stable, a distance of several hundred feet. Meanwhile, a record-breaking 500 guests crowded the piazza and dining hall of the Appledore Hotel at the Isles of Shoals. Portsmouth, a Boston newspaper noted, was fast becoming the "Weimar of America," comparing New Hampshire's only port to the historic, cultural, and influential German city.

BELOW: *First opened by Thomas and Eliza Laighton in 1848, the Appledore House drew summer visitors out of sweltering, polluted American cities to the cool "healthy air" of the Isles of Shoals, just a short ferry ride from the Port of Portsmouth. (ATH)*

The Temple, at its peak, had been a workable theater with a "set of scenery," a drop curtain, and a functioning stage. Towards its end, like the ill-fated Cameneum nearby, the walls and ceiling shimmered with decorative painting, and there was even a "bowling salon" on the ground floor. But despite major renovations and four different owners, it was always a repurposed wooden church that featured sober, wholesome, and enlightening presentations. The Music Hall, "devoted exclusively to entertainments," was a new thing entirely.

A larger, sturdier, and more attractive seventy-five by 103-foot structure began to appear. Sometimes described as Romanesque or "approaching the Gothic," the square exterior front, with its five matching stone bays, more closely follows the Italianate style of architecture popular at the time. Its sixteen-inch-thick brick walls rose from a stone foundation three to four feet wide towards a slate hip roof forty feet above the street. Ten windows lined the Chestnut Street entrance with fourteen more along Warren (now Porter) Street. A vestibule flanked by a broad

ABOVE: *Already included in this 1877 bird's-eye view map of Portsmouth, the Music Hall can be seen at the corner of Chestnut and Warren (now Porter) streets. The seventy-five-foot tall back stage addition was not part of the original structure. (JDR)*

stairway led to a seventy-two-foot main hall with a central ticket office, cloakroom, and usher's station.

"A liberal outlay of money," the newspaper reported without mentioning the Peirce family by name, allowed architect William Ashe to create his masterpiece. "Too much praise cannot be awarded to him," the *Morning Chronicle* editor concluded in January 1878 as the Music Hall prepared to open. Amazingly, no photographs of the theater's early days have been found. So we must rely on the newspaper's detailed description as our guided tour of the original Music Hall interior. It was lit by 230 gas lamps connected by up to 3,000 feet of piping. A glass chandelier crafted in Rhode Island hung from the ornate ceiling. A steam boiler in the basement provided blessed blasts of heat in winter.

Opening night welcome

A week before the official premiere the *Daily Evening Times* announced that tickets could be obtained at Preston's Drug Store downtown. Out-of-towners who placed orders with Mr. Preston by mail were obliged to pick up their tickets early, or they would be resold. Within half an hour of their release, seventy-five tickets — priced at seventy-five, fifty, and thirty-five cents — were gone. A full house was predicted.

It was seventy-eight-year-old W.H.Y. Hackett, now father-in-law of banker Robert Peirce, who addressed the first Music Hall audience on January 29, 1878. Hackett congratulated the city for its "beautiful, commodious, much-needed and long-expected" new theater.

And before the curtain rises at the Music Hall, we should pause to take the measure of the man upon the stage. While the Peirce family chose to work in near obscurity behind the scenes, W.H.Y. Hackett — who would not survive the summer of 1878 — had played out his life in the public eye. As the oldest working attorney in Rockingham County, he was a relic of another age. But he also foreshadowed the selfless, steady, community-oriented citizens of Portsmouth who would step up and save the endangered theater a century later, and who keep its doors open and its spotlights blazing to this day.

Born in 1800, only a year after George Washington's death, Mr. Hackett was the son of a farmer from Gilmanton, New Hampshire, but his love of reading compelled him to study law. He was drawn to the port city where fledgling attorneys like orator Daniel Webster and future president Franklin Pierce had cut their teeth. Inspired by the city's 1823 bicentennial celebration, a young Mr. Hackett fell in with lawyer Nathaniel A. Haven, Jr. An extraordinary figure, Haven was a founder of the Portsmouth Athenaeum, the NH Historical Society, the *Portsmouth Journal*, and the local Unitarian church. The two men became law partners in 1826. With the previously mentioned Rev. Orange Clark, an itinerant school teacher, they founded the city's Forensic Society, a debate and lecture club that evolved into the first Portsmouth Lyceum. When Nathaniel Haven died suddenly of scarlet fever that same

ABOVE: *William Henry Young Hackett (1800-1878) was a prominent Portsmouth lawyer and banker, best remembered today for his stirring speech at the opening of the Music Hall delivered a few months before his death. (JDR)*

year, Hackett dedicated himself to the solo practice of the law for the next half century. With his wife Olive, a descendant of the venerable Pickering family, they built a house and raised their children on Congress Street, just across the city's main artery from the wealthy Peirce clan.

Inspired by his lost law partner, Hackett threw himself into reviving both the culture and the economy of his adopted city — building bridges, establishing a library, improving schools. As a state senator and representative for the conservative Whig party, he helped tie Portsmouth to the expanding railroad network, connecting the old port south to Boston, north to Portland, westward to the state capital at Concord, and to the popular White Mountain resorts beyond. He was instrumental in establishing the country's first National Bank at Portsmouth. Hackett then joined forces with his neighbor Ichabod Goodwin, New Hampshire's Civil War governor, to supply President Lincoln with badly needed troops and supplies during the bloody conflict. Hackett's house, after his death, became the city's first YMCA.

"To be happy," Hackett once told a friend, "one must make himself useful." His multiple careers, according to his biographer, often created financial opportunities, but Hackett never sought wealth for its own sake. Instead, he saw his powerful positions as opportunities "to do good in the world." So we can only imagine the pride that the Hon. W.H.Y. Hackett felt as he surveyed the audience, packed with familiar faces, in the majestic new theater that had literally risen from the ashes of the Temple, where he had attended countless lectures and temperance meetings. Still active and energetic, the man with the thick hair and youthful complexion stood to his full six feet at the lectern. Only a slight paunch betrayed his advanced years.

"A community is known," he said as if clairvoyant, "by the character and place of its amusements." The more often a community comes together in that "well ordered place," Hackett predicted, the more connected that community would grow. "We cannot, in company and sympathy enjoy music and the drama— those recreations which enliven, sweeten, and lengthen life — without increasing our interest in and our respect for each other," Hackett concluded. Then he stepped quietly off the stage and into the misty annals of local history.

ABOVE: *The Hackett and Peirce families were nineteenth-century neighbors on Congress Street in downtown Portsmouth. The home of W.H.Y. Hackett was repurposed into the city's first YMCA. It was moved to a nearby site in 1903 to make way for a new YMCA building, then demolished under urban renewal in 1969. (ATH)*

The curtain rises

What followed Mr. Hackett's speech was state of the art. The first Music Hall production, according to a fragile yellowing playbill, was a "brilliant domestic comedy" in three acts by the English playwright T.W. Robertson. The play, entitled *Caste*, revolves around a French nobleman, George D'Alroy, who falls in love with Esther Eccles, a ballet dancer far below his social status. The relationship is doomed, George's friend says, due to the "inexorable law of caste." This is the social convention, the friend explains, "that commands like to marry like, and forbids a giraffe to fall in love with a squirrel."

When George proposes marriage, even Esther protests. "What future is there for us?" she cries. "You're a man of rank, and I am a poor girl who gets her living by dancing." Esther's father, to make matters worse, is a stumbling, pandering, drunkard. Scorning tradition, the two lovers are secretly married. But in Act II George's regiment is sent off to fight in India, where he is reportedly killed in action. He's alive, of course. George returns home in Act III to discover he is a father — and all's well that ends well.

Although its plot moves slowly, its characters are dated, and its punchlines may fall flat with modern viewers, *Caste* has found its way into theater history. Released in 1867, it was performed 650 times on the London stage, where it has been revived off and on to the present day. It was translated to film in 1915 and again in 1930, and later resurrected as a BBC television play.

Although mild by modern standards, the "problem plays" of dramatist T.W. Robertson were innovative, even shocking, to Victorians. *Caste,* for example, took on the very real issue of social prejudice by satirizing conventional views about class and marriage. At the finale George D'Alroy exclaims, "Nobody's nobody. Everybody's somebody . . . What brains may break through, love may leap over."

Robertson is also remembered for his naturalistic staging style in which characters moved and spoke as if in real life, rather than in the exaggerated, melodramatic way audiences were used to. His characters chatted about everyday topics and moved around on uncomplicated sets that mirrored actual rooms. Robertson's "cup and saucer" dramas were also in sharp contrast

ABOVE: *With no experience in the entertainment industry, the Peirce family outsourced the opening events at the Music Hall to Boston Theatre manager Orlando Tompkins (1818-1884). Tompkins frequently worked with famed Shakespearian actor Edwin Booth. The two men were together in Boston in 1865 when they learned that Edwin's brother, John Wilkes Booth, had assassinated President Abraham Lincoln. (JDR)*

OPPOSITE: *A poster announces the play* Caste *by T.W. Robertson as performed at the Lyceum Theatre in Edinburgh, Scotland. This "brilliant domestic comedy" was the premier event at the opening of the Music Hall in 1878. (NLS)*

LEFT: *With no industry standards for stage size, it was common practice for theaters to have a series of "stock" scenes that visiting troupes could use instead of carrying the large painted drops. These usually consisted of a forest scene, a plaza or town square, and various interiors. Some theaters also included a purely decorative drop that was placed near the front of the stage and, when in view, could hide scene changes happening behind it. At the Music Hall* The Choice of a Model *painted by Mariano Fortuny y Carbó was reproduced by Manchester, New Hampshire, painter E.H. MacAndrews in 1901 for the grand re-opening under Frank Jones. The fate of the painted curtain is unknown. (NAG)*

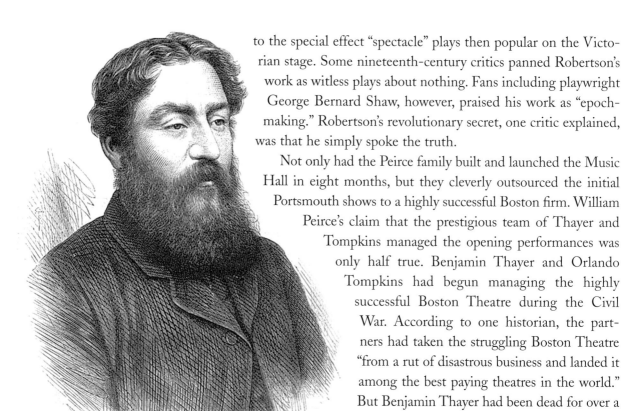

to the special effect "spectacle" plays then popular on the Victorian stage. Some nineteenth-century critics panned Robertson's work as witless plays about nothing. Fans including playwright George Bernard Shaw, however, praised his work as "epoch-making." Robertson's revolutionary secret, one critic explained, was that he simply spoke the truth.

Not only had the Peirce family built and launched the Music Hall in eight months, but they cleverly outsourced the initial Portsmouth shows to a highly successful Boston firm. William Peirce's claim that the prestigious team of Thayer and Tompkins managed the opening performances was only half true. Benjamin Thayer and Orlando Tompkins had begun managing the highly successful Boston Theatre during the Civil War. According to one historian, the partners had taken the struggling Boston Theatre "from a rut of disastrous business and landed it among the best paying theatres in the world." But Benjamin Thayer had been dead for over a year by 1878, and Orlando Tompkins was slowly being replaced by a younger partner.

The full Music Hall premiere included five separate performances by a troupe of Boston actors spread over three days. The kick-off two-hour production of *Caste* on Tuesday evening was followed by a short farce titled *Mr. Wopps* about a brainless Monty Python-style policeman. The Wednesday bill featured the play *Married Life*, hyperbolically described as "the most successful comedy in the English language." It was paired with a humorous sketch called *Toodles*. Miss Mary Cary, "the ingénue actress from Boston," and Mr. Charles H. Thayer, a pantomime and comedian, were given top billing in the Portsmouth cycle of plays. Charles Thayer, for the record, also served as manager to the Irish playwright Oscar Wilde and to America's superstar actor Edwin Booth. Booth had been performing at the Boston Theatre and lodging with Orlando Tompkins when he first learned that his brother John Wilkes had killed President Lincoln.

The series culminated on Thursday evening with a lengthy five-act production of *Poor Jo*, a partial adaptation of *Bleak House*

ABOVE: *Thomas William Robertson (1829-1871), author of the comedy* Caste *was an English dramatist best remembered for his "problem plays" that treated contemporary issues honestly and realistically. (JDR)*

by Charles Dickens. A minor character in the Dickens novel, Jo is a ragged, bullied, orphaned, illiterate boy forced to sweep the manure-filled streets of London in exchange for meager handouts. One of Dickens' most pitiable characters, Jo's tragic story (he dies of pneumonia) was appealing to sentimental nineteenth-century audiences. Miss Mary Cary, who had successfully played the part of Jo in Boston and New York, reprised her role at Portsmouth's new theater, undoubtedly bringing the house to tears. The playbill promised viewers "the most realistic performance ever witnessed on the stage." Victorian theater scholar Nina Auerbach, commenting on the popularity of the play, once noted, "Long after Dickens' death, Jo continued to provide a show-case for shapely actresses."

The acting troupe from Boston was certainly impressed to find a spanking new theater in the Old Port. They were the first to see the decorative walls and colorfully painted frescoes, spacious galleries and balcony, crimson enameled cloth seats, gilt iron railings, and an enormous gas-powered chandelier that could illuminate the entire auditorium. The stage, measuring twenty-nine feet deep by thirty-five feet wide, was supported by the most modern machinery for hoisting the curtains, with an orchestra pit at the front and six dressing rooms at the back. A set of freshly painted backdrop scenery depicted a drawing room, chamber, kitchen, street, rustic landscape, and a prison. Thirty-two painted side wings included realistic rocks, trees, and a movable cottage. A crimson velvet curtain bore the image of the New Hampshire state seal. The ornamented proscenium, though not elaborate by Boston standards, was eighteen feet high and surrounded by "a design representing music."

Architect William Ashe had delivered his showpiece on time and on budget. He would create many more impressive city buildings and private homes in Portsmouth. The new theater, the *Morning Chronicle* announced, "is a model in the perfection of its every detail." Following the three-day opening extravaganza, the conservative Peirce family found themselves deeply invested in a risky new Music Hall. "We hope," the *Chronicle* editor concluded, "its public spirited proprietors may reap a fair reward for their enterprise." ❧

ABOVE: *A dramatic adaptation of Charles Dickens' novel* Bleak House *by J.P. Burnett entitled* Poor Jo *was a huge success in America. Actress Jenny Lee, who made a career out of playing the impoverished street sweeper, was the wife of the playwright. (GCC/WIK)*

CHAPTER 4

Thank you, Mr. Jones

Bigger, better, brighter

It feels hauntingly proper that the 1878 Music Hall, the source of so much joy over the last century and a half, was built on the site of so much sorrow. Originally the land was part of an expansive field or "glebe" given to the first Portsmouth minister. But in 1711 town officials selected the spot for an almshouse, where impoverished inmates struggled to work off their debt. By mid-century there was a two-story prison here, with hewn oak timbers, thick walls, stone cells, and well-spiked iron bars. A thirty-one-year-old teacher named Ruth Blay, imprisoned for concealing the death of her stillborn child, was bound in chains here for many months before she was hanged in 1768.

By 1781 the prison had been replaced by a barn behind the State Street home of Woodbury Langdon, a controversial businessman, statesman, and judge. That year a fire began in the barn, reportedly by boys trying to make clay marbles in a stove. It spread and destroyed Langdon's house. In 1795 he rebuilt a three-story brick mansion on the nearby site that locals called "the costliest house anywhere about." That home became part of the Rockingham Hotel, owned and expanded in the next century by none other than millionaire alemaker Frank Jones, who would later breathe new life into the Music Hall. Langdon's barn, meanwhile, made way for the Baptist church, later renamed the "Temple," that made way, in turn, for the city's longest surviving playhouse.

ABOVE: *By age forty, as seen here, "ale tycoon" Frank Jones (1832-1902) had already served as mayor of Portsmouth and was about to be elected a representative to the U.S. Congress from New Hampshire. He would eventually own hotels, banks, railroad lines, racing stables, an insurance company, utilities, and the Music Hall. (ATH)*

OPPOSITE: *A view of Market Square in 1900 when Hon. Frank Jones, the second owner of the Music Hall, began the renovation and expansion of the theater building (ATH)*

Following the three-day opening extravaganza in 1878, the Music Hall delivered a rapid-fire series of shows week after week, year after year. For a reasonable fee, audiences could now experience performances from Shakespeare to light opera by Gilbert & Sullivan, plus popular comedies imported from Boston and New York City, concerts, and early vaudeville acts. Lyceum-style lecturers like those at the former Temple shared the stage with local amateur talent, school recitals, political rallies, temperance meetings, benefits, community events, and sacred music on Sundays. Music Hall production manager and historian Zhana Morris has spent countless hours combing through early Portsmouth newspapers on microfilm. Her research, to date, has uncovered over 750 performances in the theater's first two decades.

Of the thousands of actors, musicians, and speakers who appeared here under the ownership of the Peirce family, one name rings out. Former pony express rider and western scout, William F. Cody, aka "Buffalo Bill," had killed 4,280 head of buffalo by the time he arrived in Portsmouth. His first two shows, probably at the Temple in 1873 and 1875, did not impress the critics. Tall and handsome on stage, Cody was, at first, a ridiculous actor in a stiff, scripted play that was "the worst acted atrocity ever seen on any stage." While a Portsmouth critic complained that the "fierce and untamed" Indians were anything but, a New York newspaper rated one Cody show "so wonderfully bad that it was almost good."

On November 15, 1878, the "Buffalo Bill Combination" returned to find Portsmouth had built a state-of-the-art Music Hall. Cody's hard-knuckle troupe — sometimes including James "Wild Bill" Hickok — again thrilled the public and appalled the critics. Their raucous, smoke-filled shows featured live horses, sharpshooting, romance, outlaws, trick roping, sham battles, and an authentic Native American "princess." Cody brought three more plays to Portsmouth with titles like *The Prairie Waif* and *Buffalo Bill's Pledge*. In 1883 Cody traded in small stages like the Music Hall for his enormous outdoor Wild West Show that featured a traveling cast and staff of up to 500 men, women, and children, plus horses and thirty surviving buffalo.

On March 22, 1883, the Music Hall welcomed Charles Sherwood Stratton, better known as General Tom Thumb, and

ABOVE: *Two of the most famous Music Hall performers of the late nineteenth century were showman William Frederick "Buffalo Bill" Cody (1846-1917) and a diminutive Charles Sherwood Stratton (1838-1883), better known as General Tom Thumb. (WIK)*

OPPOSITE: *Before expanding to huge outdoor venues, a smaller theatrical version of* Buffalo Bill's Wild West Show *drew crowds to the Temple and the Music Hall. (MIS)*

his wife Lavinia. The three-foot-tall entertainer, made world famous from childhood by showman P.T. Barnum, was not well. Having met world leaders from Abraham Lincoln to Queen Victoria, the famous Tom Thumb died of a stroke four months after his Portsmouth show. Lavinia, at two-and-a-half feet and twenty-nine pounds, went on to marry the diminutive Italian Count Primo Magri, and returned to the stage with her troupe, the Lilliputian Opera Company.

Less famous but also diminutive was Milo E. Benedict, the acclaimed "boy composer and pianist" who gave a recital at the hall around this time. Benedict, then in his teens, played compositions he had written since the tender age of seven. A surviving vintage handbill redundantly declared this work to be "the most striking exhibition of genius ever exhibited." His compositions included translating thunder, the sounds of battle, and bird songs into melodies for the pianoforte. Benedict was later accompanied by Gladys Perkins Fogg, a blind soprano from Boston. The two eventually married. Milo taught at St. Paul's School in Concord, New Hampshire, and the couple gave summer music lessons on Pleasant Street in Portsmouth.

ABOVE: *Among the popular animal acts was Prof. George Bartholmew's "Equine Paradox" in which twenty "educated horses" calculated mathematical equations and played leapfrog on the Music Hall stage. (MHC)*

OPPOSITE: *Among the earliest Music Hall presentations was an antislavery play titled* Octoroon. *The title refers to the racial identification of a person whose heritage is one-eighth black. (NLS)*

ABOVE: *Like the Kearsarge Hotel, the Kearsarge fire pumper, and Portsmouth's Kearsarge Way, the Kearsarge Flute and Drum Band was named after the sloop of war USS Kearsarge. That warship took its name from New Hampshire's Mount Kearsarge that is believed to be adapted from the Native American term "Carasarga." (SBM)*

Drama, vaudeville, & minstrelsy

The year 1883 also marked the arrival of vaudeville in Boston and its satellite towns. Middle class Americans with more leisure time and more money to spend were demanding more wholesome family entertainment. These "clean variety" shows, like the itinerant acts of the 1790s and the lyceum speakers and traveling circus acts of the mid-1800s, relied on a revolving circuit of touring performers. Vaudeville (known as "music hall" in England) mixed comics, musicians, magicians, acrobats, animal acts, freak shows, dancers, speakers, and celebrities on the same stage. Ed Sullivan would later do the same for television.

Vaudeville was in its infancy during the Peirce era. Instead of many acts on one bill, the Music Hall usually offered a wide array of sensationalist one-night acts. The medium Nellie Everett, for example, appeared to float in midair. The Dunbar Sisters performed a seance, while Professor Caldwell mesmerized volunteers plucked from the Portsmouth audience. A "celebrated wizard" named Hartz performed illusions, followed by Harry French and his "Hindoo Jugglers." From child piano prodigies to lantern slide lectures of foreign lands, each show transformed the Music Hall stage. In 1884 George Bartholomew's "Equine Paradox" included twenty trained horses that could calculate math problems, act out courtroom dramas, and leap-frog over each other. The "Tableaux Phantasma" of 1892 delivered mythical scenes "composed of living people" who could "appear, vanish and reappear in a most original and pleasing manner."

Seacoast audiences enjoyed the hit dramas and comic operas of the era. Actress Maude Adams, for instance, appeared here in the title role of *Peter Pan*, which she enacted over 1,500 times in her career. Born Maude Ewing Adams Kiskadden in 1872 she first played the Music Hall at age six. A Mormon, gay, female actor in what could be a very difficult business, Maude Adams reportedly earned up to a million dollars annually at the peak of her fame. Retiring from the stage, she went on to work with engineers at General Electric where she helped design better theater lighting. Adams also collaborated with Eastman Kodak to develop improved color photography.

TOP: *Wire walkers, magicians, and hypnotists were among the most popular stage acts of the era. (JDR)*

BOTTOM: *Maude Adams (1872-1953) as Peter Pan. (WIK)*

Joseph Jefferson, another Victorian star, appeared in the stage version of *Rip Van Winkle*, adapted from the Washington Irving story about a man who fell asleep for twenty years. Jefferson played the same character for four decades, long enough to record a number of the scenes onto film in 1896. Portsmouth-born actor Henry Clay Barnabee sang the memorable role of Sir Joseph Porter in Gilbert and Sullivan's hugely popular HMS *Pinafore*, that has been staged at least a dozen times at the Music Hall. Barnabee returned as the Sheriff of Nottingham in the comic opera *Robin Hood*, a role he dominated on the American stage through 2,000 performances.

Then there was Neil Burgess, who starred as "Widow Bedott" in 1881. Burgess is best remembered today as a vaudeville comedian and female impersonator. He often played "old widdy women," a comic stereotype, wearing granny glasses and a calico shawl. Long before crossdressing comics Milton Berle and the cast of Monty Python, Burgess gained popular praise and critical respect and was among the highest paid actors of his time.

Another early variety format, popular in Portsmouth from the mid-1700s, was pantomime. Shows like the oft-repeated *Humpty Dumpty* were aimed at children and involved audience participation. Evolved from the British pantomime, these variety shows might include a trapeze artist, clowns, nursery rhyme characters, and songs, with a few mildly adult jokes tossed over the heads of children to their parents. Portsmouth audiences likewise cheered and wept to at least a dozen different productions of *Uncle Tom's Cabin*, adapted from Harriet Beecher Stowe's best-selling abolitionist novel.

As many as 400 traveling companies staged versions of the famous "Tom Show" from the 1850s to the early twentieth century. Over time the anti-slavery message was muted by special effects including floating angels, blackface minstrels, and live dogs chasing barefoot runaways across the stage. One production staged at the Music Hall promised a supporting cast of "30 colored children" happily dancing and singing against the painted backdrop of a southern plantation.

But there's no running from the truth. The most popular form of mass entertainment in America in the late 1800s was blackface minstrelsy. White actors and musicians, their faces blackened with burnt cork or greasepaint, were as familiar to audiences as television sitcoms or rock and roll today. A typical show opened with dancing, joking, and singing, followed by slapstick routines, a "plantation skit," or a parody of a popular stage play. During the two decades that the Peirce family owned the Music Hall, at least thirty different minstrel groups were hired. Companies like Duprez & Benedict's Gigantic Minstrels filled the stage. Other troupes described themselves as mammoth, mastodon, monster, magatherian, or gigantean and could include up to one hundred cast members.

Portsmouth, like all maritime cities north or south, had included black residents from its founding days. New Hampshire's first printing press operator Primus Fowle, bakers Pomp and Candace Spring, musicians Prince and Cuffee Whipple, and others earned respect from white citizens as they emerged from slavery in the late eighteenth century. The rise of blackface performers in the 1820s-1840s, historians note, was at one level an homage to African music and dancing that was more rhythmic, livelier, more original, more heartfelt, more tuneful, and therefore more entertaining than what white audiences were used to. But it came freighted with mocking and hurtful stereotypes.

After the Civil War blackface minstrelsy spread into newly-built theaters like the Music Hall where it was accepted as wholesome family entertainment. Its racist stereotypes became embedded in popular culture. As segregation and lynching expanded in the Jim Crow South, northern audiences applauded the antics of "Old Zip Coon." While even Abraham Lincoln and Mark Twain expressed a fondness for the genre, former slave Frederick Douglass pulled no punches. He called blackface minstrels "the filthy scum of white society, who have stolen from us a complexion denied them by nature . . . to make money and pander to the corrupt taste of their white fellow citizens."

Troupes of black minstrels, usually with white managers, also performed at the Music Hall. These black groups were often billed as "true Ethiopian" or "all-colored" or "jubilee" acts. They offered more authentic versions of "Negro songs," some by African American composers. The Original Georgia Minstrels,

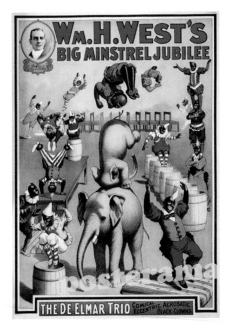

ABOVE: *White minstrels and comedians in blackface like George H. Primrose (1852–1919) were among the most frequent acts at the Music Hall. (HTC/WIK)*

ABOVE: *Despite the predominance of white minstrels in racist blackface makeup playing stereotyped versions of "negro music," Portsmouth audiences were also introduced to troupes of authentic African American performers including the Original Georgia Minstrels. (HTC/WIK)*

popular in Portsmouth, were unique in that their founder and manager, Charles B. Hicks, was a light-skinned black. Billed as "The Only Simon-Pure Negro Troupe in the World," their success and international tours led the way for other black minstrels to make a living. Hicks' players, however, were sometimes branded as "race traitors" by their peers for pandering to white audiences. The Original Georgia Minstrels were welcomed onto the Portsmouth stage, but still banned from patronizing local hotels and restaurants even into the twentieth century.

The first manager

We have only a vague sketch of John O. Ayers who booked all these shows as manager of the Music Hall during its first two decades. Like the Peirce family members who hired him, Ayers came from old Portsmouth stock, married locally, and stayed out of the limelight. From the outset, Ayers quickly faced competition. In 1879, the old Franklin Hall, located a stone's throw from the Music Hall on Congress Street, burned to the ground. Rumors quickly spread that someone planned to build a new hall in its place, causing one newspaper to quip, "Can't see why we need another."

But that same year a massive new brick Franklin Block quickly rose on the spot. It initially included two public stages, one known as The Franklin Theatre. Naming himself the "agent" of the Music Hall, Ayers quickly staked his claim as the number one venue in town. He purchased a promotional listing in a national directory of theaters, opera houses, and lecture halls. The Music Hall, he said, offered a larger stage than the Franklin Theatre, plus ample dressing rooms, a full complement of scenery, and a seating capacity of 1,200 (300 more than the Franklin). Ayers offered his superior venue for a rental fee of $55 per night, with a ticket seller, stage hands, and ushers included.

ABOVE: *Replacing the old Franklin Hall, the monumental Franklin Block was built soon after the Music Hall and contained a competing theater. The Arcadia cinema was later located here in the early twentieth century. (ATH)*

The high quality and quantity of shows at the Music Hall, a local editor speculated, might account for fewer Portsmouth-area residents traveling to see shows in the Boston area. But within a few years, Ayers was also challenged by heavily attended events at the Wentworth Hotel in nearby New Castle. Hundreds of bicycles could be seen scattered across the lawn of the richly renovated hotel during summer band concerts and "hop" dances. Wealthy businessman and politician Frank Jones, who owned the Wentworth and many other Portsmouth companies, would also take over the Music Hall by the end of the century.

John Ayers was a good manager in a rapidly changing world. He kept his head down, stayed abreast of popular trends in entertainment, and filled seats. Then, as today, the Music Hall stage was also a gathering place for the community. In 1884, for instance, Portsmouth honored the survivors of the Greely Party with a parade and a reception at the Music Hall. This scientific research team had been stranded and abandoned in the Arctic near the North Pole for three grueling years. Only six of twenty-four men returned and had been recuperating at the Portsmouth Naval Shipyard. The expedition leader, Adolphus Greely, was a Civil War hero from Newburyport, Massachusetts. The men were feted as heroes in Portsmouth, but rumors of cannibalism among the survivors dogged "Eat-em-alive Greely" for the rest of his life.

By the 1890s Thomas Edison was determined to make moving pictures as popular as his phonograph had made recorded sound. Edison's first crude films ran for only seconds and showed jugglers, dancers, a muscle man, boxers, a trapeze artist, and Annie Oakley shooting targets. These mini-movies could only be viewed through a peephole one person at a time, and yet, by the mid-1890s, arcade parlors with rows of Kinetoscopes were popping up in large cities.

A local newspaper claims that the first moving pictures seen in Portsmouth were exhibited at the Music Hall on February 17, 18, and 19 in 1898. The *Portsmouth Herald* identified Edison's latest moving picture device — "the marvel of the age" — as a Graphoscope. That is unlikely. A graphoscope was a magnifying glass, common in many households, used to view early photographs, not a complex "moving picture machine" as advertised.

ABOVE: *Rescued after three years stranded at the North Pole, Adolphus Greely (1844-1935) and the surviving members of his Arctic exploration team recuperated at the Portsmouth Naval Shipyard. The men were honored in a Portsmouth parade and a ceremony at the Music Hall. (MIS)*

Was the Edison Company trying to convince manager Ayers to install a row of Kinetoscopes in the Music Hall lobby? If so, Ayers wisely deferred. The profitable single-user Kinetoscope fad was already waning by 1898, and Edison was coming around to the idea that the big money was in projecting big movies onto big screens for big audiences.

More likely Portsmouth audiences paid twenty-five to thirty-five cents that weekend to watch clips miraculously projected on a screen using a Vitascope, a machine licensed by, but not invented by Edison. Originally called a "Phantoscope," the Vitascope was powered by electricity and cast images using light much like modern projectors. But real movies like Edison's first twelve-minute masterpiece, *The Great Train Robbery* were still in the future.

ABOVE: *Music Hall audiences likely saw their first moving picture in 1898 projected on screen using a Vitascope, a device promoted and sold, but not invented by, Thomas Edison. (LOC/WIK)*

In 1898 local gossip revealed that George Dixon would make a surprise appearance at the Music Hall. Born in Nova Scotia in 1870 and nicknamed "Little Chocolate," at five-feet, three-inches tall and eighty-seven pounds, Dixon was the first African American and first Canadian to earn a world boxing title. Having won both Bantamweight and Featherweight titles, he formed the George Dixon Specialty Company, a vaudeville act for which he is credited with creating the art of shadowboxing onstage.

Several hundred fight fans, according to the local newspaper, sat through a two-hour burlesque entitled *The Sporty Widow*, in hopes of seeing "the prominent colored pugilist." But when the band packed up and the footlights went out, irate fans realized they had been fooled. Dixon was not coming. A local reporter picks up the story from here:

> "Fake" cried somebody in the rear of the house. "Youse is lobsters," piped a small boy in the gallery and it began to ooze through the gray matter in the heads of the disgusted sports fans that they had been duped.

In a newspaper article entitled "Hamlet without Hamlet" the anonymous reporter noted wryly that men who would drop a $50 or $100 wager on a fight were suddenly incensed at having lost thirty-five cents on a theater ticket. But no one blamed manager John O. Ayers for starting the rumor in order to sell seats at the Music Hall, the reporter concluded. Ayers, too, had apparently been taken in by the hoax. And despite the absence of George Dixon, shadowboxing soon became a popular vaudeville event in Portsmouth.

John Ayers would not live to see the rise of motion pictures or shadowboxing. He died early the following year in 1899. His brief obituary reveals, in addition to the stressful job at the Music Hall, he was also superintendent of the Portsmouth Water Works and the newly elected president of a local men's club. Ayers' sudden departure and the arrival of his replacement became a pivotal moment in the history of the theater. Ambitious, verbose, shrewd, and politically connected, Fernando W. Hartford would push the manager's role to new heights.

ABOVE: *Rumors that bantamweight and featherweight champion George Dixon (1870-1908) would demonstrate his shadowboxing skills on the Music Hall stage turned out to be a false alarm. (WIK)*

The second manager

With Ayers gone and the Music Hall greatly in need of a make-over, the original owners were ready to exit the entertainment business. The Peirce family, John Ayers' widow, and the surviving theater trustee willingly turned over their stock to the wealthiest man in town. Frank Jones, a former Portsmouth mayor and New Hampshire congressman, had begun his business career selling rags, then stoves, then beer. By 1899, Portsmouth's "ale tycoon" controlled a small empire including hotels, a bank, racing stables, an insurance company, a telephone and electric utility, factories, and a sizeable interest in the local railroad.

In July 1899 the newspaper joyously reported the consummation of the sale to the honorable Mr. Jones. "Portsmouth To Have a Modern Theatre Which It Has Long Needed," the headline announced. Jones, aged sixty-six, promised to "completely renovate the house." The sale to Jones, the newspaper predicted

BELOW: *Portsmouth's wealthiest and most powerful man, Frank Jones made a career out of buying small businesses, adding enormous value, finding good managers, advertising widely, and turning a profit. His brewery at Portsmouth's West End was among the largest in the nation. (ATH)*

FRANK JONES' BREWERY & MALT HOUSES.
PORTSMOUTH, N.H.
DEPOT 82 & 84 WASHINGTON ST. BOSTON.

"will be applauded by the public generally." The ebullient owner of the newspaper, by the way, was F.W. Hartford, who was also the new manager of the Music Hall.

Born in upstate New York around 1870 and transplanted to Manchester, New Hampshire, young Hartford epitomized the "Horatio Alger" model of a poor tough kid who struggled his way to success through hard work. A street peddling newsboy at ten and a "printer's devil" at thirteen, Hartford so impressed the *Manchester Union* newspaper that he was sent to Portsmouth at age sixteen. For nine dollars a week, the plucky teenager's job was to report local news and beef up circulation in the seacoast region of the state. Hartford also worked at the Portsmouth Naval Shipyard. By 1890 he was married to Elizabeth Downing of Eliot, Maine.

Legend says Fernando Wood Hartford attracted the attention of Frank Jones who loaned the young man $2,000 (some say half that amount, but still a princely sum in 1891) to purchase the *Penny Post*. There was no pretension to fair and balanced reporting in the Gilded Age and Hartford pushed to expand the scrappy four-page daily that sold for a penny. His Portsmouth rival, the *Morning Chronicle* lambasted Hartford as having "a lump of diseased tissue that serves him as a brain." Hartford fought back. He brought legal action for the insult, and by the following year, F.W. had taken control of the daily *Chronicle* and its sister weekly, the *New Hampshire Gazette*.

In 1897 F.W. Hartford launched the *Portsmouth Herald*. His new daily pledged "more local news than all other dailies combined" and claimed to be "the family favorite." The *Penny Post* disappeared, but Hartford continued to run the *Chronicle* and the *Gazette*. Eventually, he would buy up and shut down all six of the city's newspapers, leaving only the *Portsmouth Herald* that continues to this day. So when Portsmouth newspapers covered the Music Hall for at least the next three decades, it is a safe bet that F.W. Hartford was in control of the message. He would go on, as we shall see, to become both the owner of the theater and the mayor of the city.

In September 1899, now owned by Frank Jones, the remodeled Music Hall opened for its twenty-first season. As editor of the *Portsmouth Herald* and manager of the theater, Hartford was able to simultaneously malign the late John Ayers while

ABOVE: *The enormous seventy-five-foot-tall backstage wall of the 1901 addition with its huge doors opening onto the alley at Porter Street, where countless thousands of performers have entered the Music Hall. Jones' addition turned a lovely Victorian theater building into one of the best live performance venues in New England — and now one of the oldest. (JDR)*

OPPOSITE: *Frank Jones cleverly branded his own name onto every bottle, keg, and sign that his brewery distributed across the Eastern United States (top). His mansion on Woodbury Avenue (bottom), a portion of which still stands, was situated on acres and acres of decorative gardens even though the Jones family occupied it for only a single month each summer. (ATH)*

praising his new boss. The relaunch, F.W. wrote, was attended by a record 1,500 people. The theater had been scrubbed and painted, brighter lights added, and the dressing rooms and ladies' toilets made more comfortable while the stage had been repaired, sanded, and leveled.

Acting companies would no longer come to Portsmouth "with a dread," Hartford editorialized. The *Herald* article continued:

> Ladies may now enter the foyer without fear of collecting peanut shells, cigar ends and other choice bric-a-brac on their skirts. For about the first time in its history, Music Hall is clean from the roof to the dug out under the stage . . . [The gallery] is now a respectable place for respectable people. Vulgarity and boisterousness have been abolished.

ABOVE: *The Music Hall we know today owes much of its success to the expanded backstage and the decorative touches paid for by Frank Jones, including the gilded proscenium arch and opera boxes. (DJM)*

In upcoming issues, as the twentieth century loomed, Hartford continued to hammer home this message as if it were news in order to increase ticket sales in his sparkling clean theater. He even moved upbeat Music Hall theater reviews to the front page stressing the "wholesomeness" of the productions. At long last, the *Herald* commented, "the better class of theater-goers" were buying seats in the balcony. Thanks to the benevolence of Mr. Jones, the editor implied, the upper gallery, once the domain of hoodlums, had become a first-class vantage point for watching plays and concerts. "No rowdiness or dirt is tolerated any longer," the paper reported. But Mr. Jones was just getting started. His best and final act was soon to come.

Supersize me

Not everyone welcomed the twentieth century with its onslaught of labor-saving gadgets. What seemed like science fiction in the steam-powered Victorian era was suddenly real. Flying machines, submarines, and mass-produced motorcars were on their way. Electric-powered appliances, motion pictures, neon and fluorescent lights, elevators, trolleys, and radios soon appeared. Critics worried that the avalanche of affordable Kodak Brownie cameras, home telephones, and personal talking machines might signal the demise of polite human society. But it was too late. Change was the new order of things.

Frank Jones was a large man with a reputation for thinking big. He had transformed the boxy little Wentworth Hotel into one of the largest and grandest summer resorts on the Atlantic coast. The 1,000-acre grounds surrounding his Portsmouth mansion, known as Maplewood Farms, were a wonderland of ponds, bridges, statuary, stables, gardens, and imported trees. His brick brewery in the city's West End once produced a quarter million barrels of beer annually. It is now a thriving fifteen-acre complex of shops, offices, condos, and eateries.

The 1899 Music Hall improvements were merely cosmetic. Then in 1901 Jones purchased a small slice of land used as a stable in an alley, now called Porter Street and once known as Prison Lane. Located directly behind the theater, the property was only

ABOVE: *Frank Jones was already quite ill when he purchased the Music Hall in 1899, but rumors of his death were premature. (ATH)*

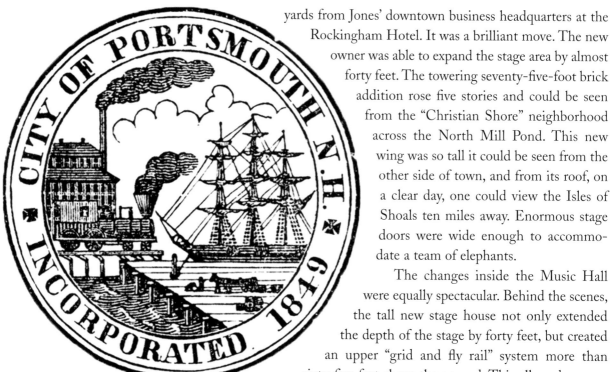

yards from Jones' downtown business headquarters at the Rockingham Hotel. It was a brilliant move. The new owner was able to expand the stage area by almost forty feet. The towering seventy-five-foot brick addition rose five stories and could be seen from the "Christian Shore" neighborhood across the North Mill Pond. This new wing was so tall it could be seen from the other side of town, and from its roof, on a clear day, one could view the Isles of Shoals ten miles away. Enormous stage doors were wide enough to accommodate a team of elephants.

The changes inside the Music Hall were equally spectacular. Behind the scenes, the tall new stage house not only extended the depth of the stage by forty feet, but created an upper "grid and fly rail" system more than sixty-five feet above the ground. This allowed scenery and curtains to be stored, hovering above the stage, then dropped quickly for even the most sophisticated productions. A hand-cranked elevator now delivered actors to tiny dressing rooms stacked four levels high at stage left. The result was a fully professionalized backstage that rivaled any New England theater outside of Boston. This upgrade, the new manager was keenly aware, not only made the Music Hall attractive to top acts at the height of the vaudeville craze, but elevated Portsmouth as a desirable destination for tourists, business owners, and new residents. The city's population, Hartford predicted, might even double.

The icing on the cake was the ornate new proscenium archway, glittering with gold leaf, that frames the stage to this day. Jones' designers actually reduced the size of the original orchestra pit and added two-story orchestra boxes to the right and left of the renovated stage. The decorative columns and plasterwork, lovingly restored in the twenty-first century, include oak leaves, a lion's head, and winged cherubs, painted by the same artist Jones hired to decorate his Wentworth by the Sea hotel nearby. The leering face at the peak of the proscenium has been described

ABOVE: *The City of Portsmouth seal representing the flourishing shipbuilding, manufacturing, and booming transportation of the Victorian Era. (JDR)*

as the Greek hero Dionysus (aka the Roman Bacchus), the god of wine and patron of the dramatic arts. Others have called him Janus, god of transitions, time, doorways, and passages, but that character is usually depicted with two heads. But in Portsmouth, among the staff of the Music Hall, the bearded figure is affectionately known as "Frank."

In 1901, approaching his seventieth birthday, Frank Jones was very busy and very ill. Despite debilitating bouts of kidney trouble, later diagnosed as Bright's disease, Jones drove himself relentlessly from one business deal to the next. The secret of his success, beyond a shark-like ability to strike hard and strike often, was hiring the best developers and the most loyal and efficient managers. Constantly on the move, Jones traveled from the West Coast to Europe to Canada, maintaining homes in Florida and Maine and rarely staying at his Portsmouth mansion for more than a month or two in the summer. With only months to live, Jones was purchasing hotels in Boston and developing a paper mill in Portsmouth.

Why Frank Jones invested in the Music Hall remains a topic of speculation. The rumor that he hoped to create a theatrical venue for his longtime mistress doesn't hold water. Others suggest Jones hoped to advance the career of his adopted daughter, Emma Sinclair, who was an amateur opera singer. More likely, the tycoon known as "Mr. Portsmouth" was influenced by the young editor F.W. Hartford. The deteriorating theater, Hartford complained in his newspaper (begun with a loan from Jones), was losing its ability to attract big acts from Boston and New York. Both were self-made men and lifelong boosters

BELOW: This antique Frank Jones Homestead Ale metal serving tray and other branded items are popular with modern collectors. (ATH)

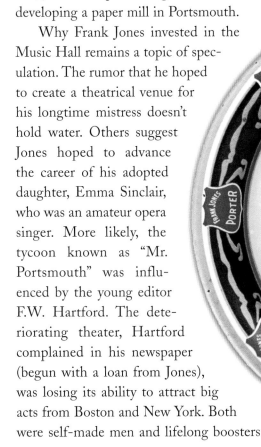

of their adopted city. And while Frank Jones, a billionaire by modern standards, was not a very charitable man, he profited himself — and the city of Portsmouth — each time he added a new building or resurrected a dying business.

While Frank Jones is credited with creating the Music Hall as we know it, the 1901 renovation was a minor project on his final to-do list. In his 460-page biography, *Frank Jones: King of the Alemakers*, historian Raymond Brighton scarcely mentioned Jones' connection to the Music Hall. In 1901, Brighton noted, the powerful men surrounding Jones were busy tamping down rumors that their wealthy boss was in poor health. The *New York Times* made that difficult. On January 19, 1902, the Times published a front page article headlined "Frank Jones is Dying." The end of New Hampshire's "Uncrowned King," the paper reported "is but a matter of a few days."

True to his nature, however, Jones did not comply. He survived nine more months before officially dying on October 2, 1902. And true to his nature, F.W. Hartford devoted the entire front page of the next *Portsmouth Herald* to honoring the man who kickstarted his career. Jones' death, Hartford wrote, "cast a shadow of gloom over Portsmouth which will be long in lifting." Jones' funeral three days later was the greatest outpouring of respect for any Portsmouth citizen in history, one newspaper claimed. The barefoot farm boy from Barrington turned robber baron was laid to rest at Harmony Grove Cemetery beneath a twenty-nine-foot-tall tombstone, the tallest in Portsmouth, that Jones had purchased for himself. The trustees of Jones' estate quickly assembled to determine the future of his extensive holdings. Without the wealthy Peirce family or Frank Jones' deep pockets, the fate of the Music Hall was suddenly in question. ❧

ABOVE: *A decorative arch built on Middle Street by members of the local Masonic Lodge for the city's Tercentennial Celebration. (ATH)*

Telluride by the Sea

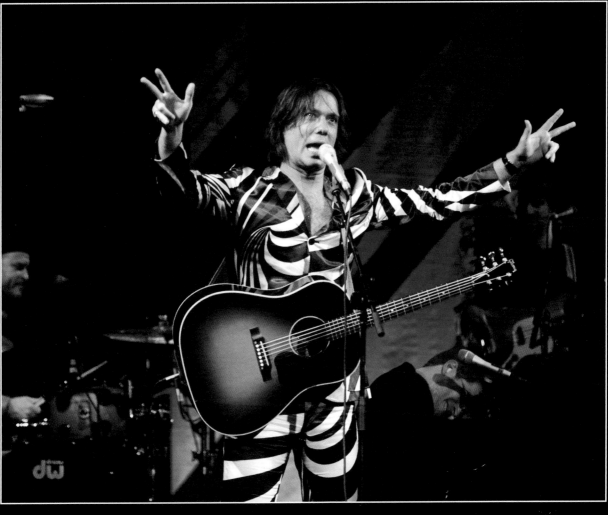

Rufus Wainwright

Gladys Knight

Tinariwen

Trevor Noah

Ladysmith Black Mambazo members

k.d. lang

Salman Rushdie

Steve Martin and the Steep Canyon Rangers

Lincoln Center Jazz Orchestra with Wynton Marsalis

Dan Zanes

National Acrobats of China

Circo Comedia

Dan Brown

Dawn Lewis aka "Peaches Mahoney" performs with Vaud and the Villains

Soweto Gospel Choir

CHAPTER 5

Vaudeville vs. Cinema

Heyday of the Portsmouth Theatre Company

If you want something done, the old saying goes, give it to a busy person. In Portsmouth in 1903, that person was Calvin Page. A former city mayor, Page was a judge, president of Granite State Fire Insurance, and newly elected to the U.S. House of Representatives. As the executor of Frank Jones' vast empire, Page was also tasked with selling off the late tycoon's hotels, utilities, and companies — including the newly renovated Music Hall.

Within days of Jones' death, F.W. Hartford joined Calvin Page in his office. For $8,000 Hartford bought all rights from the Jones' estate to three Portsmouth newspapers — the *Herald*, the *Chronicle*, and the *Gazette*. The sale included files, appliances, furniture, metal type, and a printing press, but not the electric motor to run the press or the downtown newspaper office building.

With Jones and his deep financial pockets gone, Hartford seemed to struggle with his role as manager of the theater and what to do next. He desperately wanted to brand the Music Hall as a moral, upscale venue in a visitor-friendly city. Unfortunately Portsmouth was also a tough military seaport known for its rowdy bars and alluring prostitutes. He appeared torn between putting on a smiley face and raising the alarm. One day the Music Hall

ABOVE: *A young Calvin Page (1845-1919) who became the go-to attorney for the enormous estate of the late Portsmouth millionaire Frank Jones. (ATH)*

OPPOSITE: *Long before the classic Judy Garland film, the novel* The Wonderful Wizard of Oz *(1900) by L. Frank Baum was adapted for the theater. A touring version as depicted here was performed at the Music Hall in 1904. (NYP)*

TOP: *Fernando Wood Hartford (1872-1938) purchased the Music Hall in 1903, served multiple terms as mayor of Portsmouth, and eventually controlled all the newspapers in the city. (ATH)*

BOTTOM: *Italian opera composer Pietro Mascagni (1863-1945) was among the high-brow acts F.W. Hartford delivered to working class Portsmouth audiences. (MIS)*

was "peopled to capacity," while the next day it "may be dark all next week," he reported.

Beyond the standard minstrel shows and vaudeville acts that drew local crowds, Hartford continued to import classy performers to a town not always interested in high culture. Following an evening with Italian opera composer Pietro Mascagni, for example, Hartford's newspaper offered this conflicted review: "Music Hall [attendance] last evening was large, but not so large as it should have been, because there were a few empty seats, but still large enough to demonstrate that Portsmouth is a city of music lovers."

By April Hartford had made up his mind. The only way to guarantee quality performances was to buy the theater outright. He borrowed $10,000 from a local bank and formed the Portsmouth Theatre Company. The five trustees included Hartford and his wife Lizzie, banker and former city mayor John W. Emery and his wife Mary, plus businessman Michael J. Griffin. Born in Ireland and a Catholic, Griffin became a gravedigger and then director for a Protestant cemetery on the city's South Street. Griffin expanded his graveyard business into real estate and became quite successful.

On April 28, 1903, the trustees gathered in the law office of attorney Calvin Page and signed the papers to purchase the Music Hall from the Jones' estate. With Hartford in the lead, the three men elected themselves president, vice president, secretary, and treasurer. Two weeks later they collectively invested $8,500 into their new venture. The crisp, beautifully engraved stock certificates and hand-written record of their first meetings are now part of the Portsmouth Athenaeum collection.

In Hartford's eyes, Portsmouth was the center of the universe. In the summer of 1905 his vision briefly came true as the world suddenly focused its attention on New Hampshire's tiny seaport. Over a hundred reporters from across the globe gathered in Portsmouth to cover diplomatic talks between two warring nations. By the time President Theodore Roosevelt could convince delegates from Russia and Japan to sit down in Portsmouth, the Russo-Japanese War had claimed over 600,000 lives.

INCORPORATED UNDER THE LAWS OF THE STATE OF NEW HAMPSHIRE.

NUMBER
1

SHARES
60

Portsmouth Theatre Company

CAPITAL STOCK, $18,000.

This Certifies that *Fernando H. Hartford* is the owner of *Sixty (60)* Shares of One Hundred Dollars each of the Capital Stock of **Portsmouth Theatre Company** transferable only on the books of the Corporation by the holder hereof in person or by Attorney upon surrender of this Certificate properly endorsed.

In Witness Whereof, the said Corporation has caused this Certificate to be signed by its duly authorized officers and to be sealed with the Seal of the Corporation at Portsmouth, N. H. this 15th day of May A.D. 1903.

President.   Treasurer.

Shares $100 Each.

Calvin Page cleverly offered to feed and house the delegates from both nations in separate wings of the Wentworth Hotel (now Wentworth by the Sea), another property of Frank Jones' estate. The late Mr. Jones, in effect, paid all expenses for the history-making negotiations in exchange for free publicity, boosted by a newly installed transatlantic cable that pushed daily reports on the peace negotiations to newspapers around the globe. The resulting Treaty of Portsmouth ended the bloody war. The treaty also enhanced Portsmouth's international reputation and boosted the value of the Wentworth Hotel. Calvin Page promptly leased and later sold the now famous hotel to an outside firm for a tidy profit.

As Portsmouth's go-to newspaper editor, F.W. Hartford found himself the ringmaster of a month-long media circus

ABOVE: *Original stock certificate to the founding member of the Portsmouth Theatre Company that purchased the Music Hall from the estate of Frank Jones in 1903 and managed the theater until 1945. (ATH)*

that summer. A 1905 photograph shows Hartford posing with more than forty international journalists who covered the treaty negotiations. The reporters in the photo, many sporting fashionable Panama hats, lounge on the front steps of the Rockingham Hotel, another Frank Jones property. Hartford sits at the center of the group wearing a dark suit and striped socks. He is cradling a small dog in his lap. The Kearsarge and Rockingham hotels, located on opposite sides of the Music Hall, were fully booked with visiting newsmen from around the world. Before the photo was taken, Hartford treated all one hundred reporters to a seafood dinner on the stage of the Music Hall, followed by a free vaudeville show. In November, locals packed into the theater to gasp at silent newsreel footage of the Portsmouth Peace Treaty parade they had participated in only twelve weeks earlier.

ABOVE: President Theodore Roosevelt (center) won the 1906 Nobel Peace Prize for negotiating an end to the bloody Russo-Japanese War during the Treaty of Portsmouth signed here in 1905. In this sketch Roosevelt brokers a handshake between the Japanese Emperor and the Russian Czar. None of the three men were actually in Portsmouth during the month-long negotiations. (JDR)

First rate, first run

Although the Hartford family retained ownership of the Music Hall for the next four decades, the best of times coincides with the reign of F.W. himself from 1903 until new management took over in 1916. His timing was perfect. The beautifully redecorated proscenium arch and the expanded backstage were ideal for the heyday of traveling vaudeville troupes that now outpaced the equally large minstrel shows. Comic operas like *HMS Pinafore* continued to fill seats, as did Shakespeare plays, the unstoppable drama *Uncle Tom's Cabin*, and the latest theatrical productions imported from Boston and New York. Until the arrival of three glitzy downtown cinemas, the Music Hall was the sole destination for silent films on the Portsmouth silver screen.

ABOVE: *Newspaper editor F.W. Hartford (in center with dog) poses on the steps of the Rockingham Hotel with international correspondents attending the Treaty of Portsmouth negotiations in 1905. Hartford treated the reporters to a free dinner and vaudeville show at the Music Hall next door. (ATH)*

ABOVE: *Versions of the Gilbert & Sullivan comic opera* HMS Pinafore *and various stage adaptations of Harriet Beecher Stowe's* Uncle Tom's Cabin *were among the most repeated shows at the Music Hall during this period. (WIK)*

As manager, Hartford booked top-notch shows and hyped them endlessly in his newspapers. "Music Hall has had more first-class attractions this season than ever before in its history," he boasted the week after taking control in 1903. From opera stars to dancing bears, the Portsmouth Theatre Company delivered nonstop family entertainment. "Nothing cheap but the price" was Hartford's mantra. As silent movies gained popularity, he declared, "There's no way that any picture show can hope to equal the perfect pictures presented at this theatre as they are first-run."

Hartford's hyperbole was heartfelt. Having migrated to Portsmouth in his teens, like so many before him and since, F.W. fell in love with the "Old Town by the Sea" and its storied past. His efforts to build a small, profitable media empire were intimately tied to his dream of restoring Portsmouth to its former social and economic status. And if the city's glorious past had been magnified, whitewashed, and romanticized by time — so what? Portsmouth could always use a dose of civic pride and a burst of tourist dollars.

Although it lasted little more than a decade, Hartford's "first-rate first-run" philosophy set a high bar for the Music Hall that it would not reclaim until the dawn of the twenty-first century. Hartford's ability to promote Portsmouth as a world-class city allowed him, for instance to attract an early performance of *The Wizard of Oz.* L. Frank Baum's bestselling book, published in 1900, had been quickly adapted into a musical for the stage, first in Chicago, followed by a nine-month run in New York City in 1903. The following year, Music Hall audiences saw Dorothy, her little dog, and the Scarecrow whisked from Kansas to Oz in a spectacular onstage tornado effect. There the beloved characters met a Tin Man, a Cowardly Lion, a Wizard, and dueling witches. Instead of diminutive Munchkins, however, the original production featured a chorus-line of leggy female dancers. The iconic film version with Judy Garland would not appear until 1939, the year after Hartford's death.

Countless celebrity actors, musicians, vaudevillians, and silent movie stars performed here in the Hartford heyday. Starstruck Americans collected their portraits on tobacco cards, posters, and magazine covers. But fame, with rare exception, is fickle. "They

ABOVE: *A promotional poster for the 1903 theatrical version of* The Wizard of Oz. *(LOC/WIK)*

ABOVE: *Composer and band leader John Philip Sousa (1854-1932) was a frequent performer at the Music Hall. (USM/WIK)*

kept telling us that the famous so-and-so was about to appear," a Portsmouth resident once said of the vaudeville days, "but we had never heard of the famous-so-and-so."

Lew Dockstader, who returned year after year, was a blackface comedian in a troupe including the soon-to-be famous singer, Al Jolson. Bandleader and composer John Philip Sousa dominated the Music Hall stage at least four times during Hartford's tenure. Sousa remains notable for patriotic marches like "Stars and Stripes Forever" and "Semper Fidelis." But Sousa's popular "Liberty Bell" march is best known today as the theme song to the British television comedy *Monty Python's Flying Circus*.

In July 1908, a seventy-three-year-old Mark Twain, America's beloved storyteller, grudgingly traveled to Portsmouth by train. Dressed uncharacteristically in black, Twain spoke at the dedication of a memorial to editor and author Thomas Bailey Aldrich, whose house is now part of Strawbery Banke Museum. Despite F.W. Hartford's claim that "the coolest place in summer is Music Hall," over a thousand spectators gathered at the sweltering theater to hear Twain's eulogy to his longtime literary friend.

"They seemed to think this was a funeral I was coming to, when in point of fact it is a resurrection and an occasion of joy," Twain told the perspiring crowd. But privately, the famous writer with the shock-white hair was unimpressed by the Aldrich Memorial and the old port city. Following his brief visit to Portsmouth, Twain grumbled into his diary, "A memorial museum of George Washington relics could not excite any considerable interest if it were located in that decayed town." Twain was unmoved by the fact that his own daughter, singer Clara Clemens, had performed at the Music Hall the previous year.

Budding local philanthropist Rosamond "Aunt Rozzie" Thaxter was in the audience that night. The thirteen-year-old granddaughter of Isles of Shoals poet Celia Thaxter, Rozzie later recalled seeing Mark Twain with his shocking white hair and a bright red carnation. She had been enchanted by her first play there even though, Rozzie later recalled, it was only actors dressed in a "moth-eaten" camel suit walking through a fake dust storm in the desert. Years later, sitting in the same seats, Rozzie watched silent films starring Jean Harlow, Mary Pickford, and Douglas Fairbanks.

American author and humorist Mark Twain (Samuel Langhorne Clemens, 1835–1910) (above) grudgingly accepted a request to speak in Portsmouth at the dedication of a museum to his late friend Thomas Bailey Aldrich. Budding writer and philanthropist Rosamond Thaxter (1895–1989) (right), granddaughter of poet Celia Thaxter, was in the audience when Twain spoke at the Music Hall. Twain's daughter, singer Clara Clemens (1874–1962) (above right) had previously appeared on the same stage. (WIK/ATH)

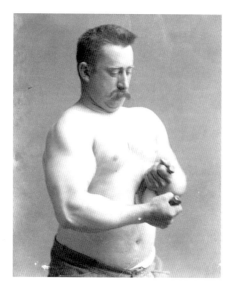

TOP: *Strongman Edward Stickney (born 1860) of Portsmouth toured widely on the vaudeville circuit. Dubbed "The American Apollo," Stickney was best known for hoisting a twelve-pound dumbbell 15,000 times in a single day. (SBM)*

BOTTOM: *Vaudeville performer King Dynamo, a wizard of electricity, was better known locally as Ernest Howard Byrnes (1883-1961), owner of Byrnes Auto Electric Service on State Street in Portsmouth. (ATH)*

A smorgasbord of talent

The theory that motion pictures suddenly killed vaudeville is too simplistic to be true. In Hartford's day, the two were equally popular and even symbiotic. At the Music Hall, everyone knew, a fresh cluster of movies was introduced on Mondays, Wednesdays and Fridays. Vaudeville shows changed every Monday and Thursday. Both offered a constant flow of ten-minute acts that varied widely.

A Navy Yard telegraph operator, Herbert Waldron, writing to his distant fiancée in 1914 said the Music Hall included two "fairly good" vaudeville acts between short movies. He also caught a film at the Scenic Temple, the only other place in town then regularly showing films. The Scenic was located in Peirce Hall on High Street across from the modern municipal parking garage and offered a dance hall on the first floor with movies on the second. Waldron's letter to his girlfriend "Spike" provides an extremely rare glance at the mash-up of silent shorts and live music:

> It was a pretty good bill and if one gets tired looking at the pictures you can watch em dance, both going on at the same time. They have a crack orchestra, which plays constantly, with practically no intermission, playing all the latest dance music, and some piano player — believe me — he can ragtime anything . . . [and] has the time and snap that make you stamp your feet.

Vaudeville performers — male and female, children and adults — represented a cross section of the immigrants streaming into the country in the twentieth century. An estimated 25,000 vaudevillians, often talented, but poorly educated, appeared on American stages. Actors delivered between five and a dozen shows daily. They also symbolized a cross section of the Irish, Greek, Russian, Italian, African-American, Jewish, and other groups that swelled the growing neighborhoods of Portsmouth.

Newspaper ads reveal a smorgasbord of live acts largely unchanged since the Victorian era. They included clog dancers, fancy rope spinners, hypnotists, magicians, regurgitators, racist "coon song" singers, and acrobats. There were lots and lots of comics, plus contortionists, yodelers, trapeze artists, bag punchers,

weight lifters, and serpentine dancers — not to mention talented bears, horses, dogs, and parrots. Unlike burlesque shows, there was no nudity, no profanity, and no overt sexual references.

No vaudeville artist wanted to perform first, as audiences were arriving, or last, as crowds were leaving the theater. Star billing was reserved for the acts just before intermission and second-to-last. Shows were paced to alternately enliven and sooth the spectators. Zeynard's Liliput-Speciality Troupe, for example, might follow Baby Patti (aka Ethel Dyffryn), billed as "The Youngest Star in the World." Dow & Dow were known as the "Hebrew Comedians," while the long forgotten Paul Jappra held the dubious title, "The World's Heaviest Wire Performer." Especially popular in Portsmouth were the "illustrated songs," played live as colorful lantern slides were projected onto a large white screen. The forerunner of music videos, illustrated songs were a clever marketing tool for selling wax and vinyl records, player piano rolls, and sheet music to the latest hit tunes.

And then there was King Dynamo. In surviving photographs, the King appears in a dark rubber raincoat with a wizard-style hood. He is wearing bulging rubber shorts. He holds a long metal rod near a massive tubular induction coil that, we can only assume, sparked and crackled like those in the laboratory of a mad movie scientist. In the real world, Ernest Howard Byrnes ran an electrical supply shop on State Street in Portsmouth. On the magical Music Hall stage, however, King Dynamo shocked audiences as he generated large, but ultimately harmless, high voltage lightning.

ABOVE: *Among the best-known local performers of his time was actor, comedian, and singer Henry Clay Barnabee (1833-1917). In his autobiography,* My Wanderings *(1913), Barnabee recounts his boyhood days in Portsmouth where his father drove a stagecoach. His extensive collection is archived at the Portsmouth Public Library and he is buried in South Cemetery. (MHS)*

Triple threat theaters

Despite F.W. Hartford's efforts to bring clean family entertainment to the Music Hall, Portsmouth was still a tough and sometimes dangerous seaport. In the summer of 1912 the city was "under siege" according to the competing *Portsmouth Times* newspaper following a series of robberies and murders in the now gentrified South End. Politicians, reporters, and police had long turned a blind eye to the many bordellos and bars that lined the waterfront. Reacting to an increasingly irate public, Portsmouth mayor Daniel Badger issued a decree to "close forthwith and permanently keep closed all houses of ill repute in this city."

Change was in the salty seacoast air. According to archived financial records 1912 was the first year that the three Music Hall trustees cashed in on their investment. Hartford, John Emery,

and Michael Griffin paid themselves checks totaling $8,500, worth roughly $200,000 today. They divided the same amount annually for the next two years. By 1915 Emery and Griffin were out. In thanks for their service, the departing trustees of the Portsmouth Theatre Company and their families were granted free admission to all shows. The surviving officers, F.W. and his wife Lizzie Hartford, were joined by their only son, Justin D. Hartford.

The buyout was aptly timed. As publisher of the city's daily newspaper, Hartford undoubtedly knew well in advance that investors were planning to construct two competing and impressive cinemas in downtown Portsmouth. The first, the Olympia, was owned by John Henry Bartlett. Like Hartford, who would eventually absorb all six Portsmouth newspapers into his daily

ABOVE: A large crowd in front of the Colonial Theatre in Market Square in the 1920s. The building, now demolished, stood near the North Church. (ATH)

Portsmouth Herald, Bartlett was about to become a local media mogul. A former school principal turned lawyer, Bartlett was the law partner of Calvin Page, executor of the Frank Jones estate, and married to Page's daughter Agnes.

Bartlett was already a key player in two local banks and two insurance companies when he purchased two lots of land on Vaughan Street, now Vaughan Mall. His "New Theatre," according to the deed, contained a projection booth permanently attached to the building. It was the city's first purpose-built cinema. With 998 plush new seats, an ornate proscenium arch, brass railings, marble stairs, and four grand opera boxes, the Olympia rivaled the aging Music Hall as a performance stage. It opened in January 1915 to a packed house. Governor Rolland

ABOVE: *The attractive interior of the Olympic Theatre, Portsmouth's first purpose-built cinema, was later converted to office space on Vaughan Mall. (ATH)*

Spaulding pushed the button that raised the curtain electrically for the first show.

Although "talking pictures" would not arrive for another decade, movies were rapidly improving. John Bartlett's ledgers, now stored at the Portsmouth Athenaeum, indicate he rented films from many distributors and hired vaudeville acts from a range of big city talent agencies. His glowing new electric sign lit up the corner of Vaughan and Congress streets. His biggest weekly expense was not talent, but electricity generated by the Rockingham County Power and Lighting Company on Daniel Street, now Harbour Place office suites.

Located only a few yards from the North Church in Market Square, the attractive new 1,200-seat Colonial Theatre opened three months after the Olympia. The opening night audience enjoyed fifteen reels of short films, a six-piece orchestra, vaudeville comics, and an acrobatic cyclist. The Colonial was owned by William P. Gray, a Colorado-born entrepreneur who married a Portsmouth woman named Mary Engen. Before migrating East, Gray had been a professional race track jockey, then managed baseball and basketball teams. With a partner, Gray also operated movie houses in Lewiston and Augusta, Maine.

Gray also ran the 400-seat Scenic Temple in Peirce Hall. The Scenic offered "photoplays." These short silent movies required a special projector, synced to a piano or organ, that could play a brief soundtrack timed to match the action on the screen. The photoplayer used perforated paper rolls, like those in a player piano, to create a "canned" soundtrack, eliminating the need for a live musician to accompany silent films. Some automated players included drums and bells, or could produce credible sound effects like wailing sirens or gunshots. Primitive by today's standards, photoplays were state-of-the-art entertainment — when they worked properly.

ABOVE: *A Portsmouth teacher turned attorney, John Henry Bartlett (1869-1952) opened the Olympia Theatre in 1915. Bartlett then organized the Allied Theatres Company that controlled the movie and vaudeville productions at all four downtown theaters, including the Music Hall. He served as governor of New Hampshire from 1919-1921. (MIS)*

"The Portsmouth Combination"

Instead of one, Portsmouth audiences suddenly had four amusement venues to choose from, located almost on top of one another in the walkable historic city center. In 1915 a battle for customers played out in the local newspapers. At first the fledgling Olympia boldly offered the "Best Pictures, Best Vaudeville." John Henry Bartlett also cut the daily matinee price at the Olympia from a dime to a nickel. The newly opened Colonial and Scenic also claimed to provide the finest vaudeville and movies. The aging Music Hall had no choice but to brand itself as "The Show That All Others Try to Imitate." Advertising revenue from all four theaters flowed into the *Portsmouth Herald* and its competitor, the *Portsmouth Times*.

With each theater offering four or five new vaudeville acts and as many films every few days, patrons could choose from as many as a hundred short performances each week. But it couldn't last. To control the city's burgeoning entertainment business, Bartlett, Gray, and his partners, "the Badger Brothers," joined forces. Their new management group, the Allied Theatres Company, would run the Olympia, Colonial, and Scenic cooperatively. Bartlett was named president.

The formation of Allied in 1916 "created considerable interest" in New England, according to *Moving Picture World*, an early trade journal. The company was created, Bartlett candidly explained, because Portsmouth's population was too small to support four full-time theaters. The inevitable result would be "unreasonable and suicidal competition," Bartlett said in a press release.

To avoid a crisis, Bartlett continued, his Allied Theatres Company would lease the Colonial and the Scenic from Mr. Gray. By mutual agreement, the "palatial" new Olympia and Colonial would become the primary cinemas in town. Major first-run movies were assigned to the Olympia while the Colonial was to be headquarters for vaudeville acts and short snappy new films. Each hall was to be supplied by different film companies. The Scenic would be opened only for "overflow" audiences and for dances.

OPPOSITE: *(top) As cinema evolved from the early Vitascope and silent shorts to "talkies," local theaters continued to alternate movies with live vaudeville acts up to the era of the Great Depression. (MIS)*

OPPOSITE: *(bottom) Downtown Portsmouth theaters, meanwhile, had to compete with the rise in popular dance music performed by groups like Bo Garland's Dance Orchestra, also known as the "Pepper Boys." Local dummer Harry "Bo" Garland and his band, seen here in the early 1920s, played at a variety of seacoast venues and in Boston. (ATH)*

Hartford continued to list himself as manager of the Portsmouth Theatre in 1915, but his glory days were over. Behind the scenes, he had cut a deal with the new management team. In 1916 and for the next two decades, John Bartlett and Allied Theatres Company leased the Music Hall from Hartford for an annual rate of $2,500. As World War I approached, the once grand Music Hall, by design, backed away from the lucrative moving picture business and focused on intermittent stage shows, political rallies, and public meetings.

It was during the end of World War I that a curious group of players took the stage, thanks to prison reformer Thomas Mott Osborne. Portsmouth Naval Prison, the hulking cement "castle" at Portsmouth Naval Shipyard in nearby Kittery, had gained a reputation for its harsh treatment of Navy inmates. Chained "lockstep" marching, striped uniforms, and forced silence were standard practice. Osborne, then prison warden, believed instead that every prisoner could be rehabilitated if treated humanely. A liberal visionary, Osborne had little respect for naval bureaucracy and briefly turned Portsmouth Prison into a model community in which convicts nearly guarded and governed themselves.

With tacit approval of Franklin Delano Roosevelt, then Assistant Secretary of the Navy, Osborne sanctioned members of the prison drama club to perform outside the walls of their jail. As many as fifty largely unsupervised prisoners — including musicians, set designers, costume and makeup artists — presented successful variety shows and a Shakespeare play at the Music Hall. They then voluntarily returned to prison without a single attempted escape. After Osborne's dismissal, however, Portsmouth Prison abandoned his experiment and returned to its legendary harsh ways.

Another unique local production brought the Music Hall briefly to life during its often locked-up period under Allied management in the 1920s. A sold-out audience cheered the Temple Israel Players in an original musical comedy called *Fresh Eggs*. The story took place in the distant future of 1999 A.D. where a pair of inventive poultry merchants developed hens that could each produce 900 eggs per day. Between scenes specialty acts included a whistling solo, a number by the Whispering Saxes, and a dance by young ladies dressed as fairies. The Temple Israel

ABOVE: *Near "suicidal competition" between four downtown theaters led to the formation of the Allied Theatres Company, managed by New Hampshire governor John Bartlett. (JDR)*

fundraiser featuring members of the Portsmouth Jewish community was so successful that it ran a second night. It also inspired a later operetta by the Council of Jewish Juniors presented entirely in Yiddish.

Theater manager John H. Bartlett, meanwhile, was moving up. In 1918, as World War I ended, Bartlett was elected governor of New Hampshire. That same year, Fernando Wood Hartford began flexing his own political muscles. He was, after all, named after New York City Mayor Fernando Wood, head of the infamous Tammany Hall political machine. With the Portsmouth Naval Shipyard fueling the seacoast economy, F.W. made a wild prediction. In an article in the *Granite Monthly*, he claimed that postwar Portsmouth would soon double its population and outstrip Manchester as New Hampshire's manufacturing capital.

"For thirty years I have been shouting to our citizens," Hartford wrote, Portsmouth was about to become "the largest city in the state."

Shipbuilding, however, sloughed off after the war and today the population of Manchester is five times larger than Portsmouth. Despite his failed predictions, Hartford was elected mayor of his beloved city in 1921. Through the Roaring Twenties and into the Depression Era of the 1930s, he served a record-breaking seven terms in office.

With others responsible for the mostly inactive Music Hall, life was good for the Hartfords. Candid pictures from the family scrapbook show them vacationing aboard cruise ships and summering at their cottage on nearby Rye Beach. They moved into an upscale Portsmouth home on Miller Avenue. Son Justin "Juddy" Hartford, flourished at the United States Naval Academy in Annapolis, Maryland. Daughter Emma graduated from the elite Smith College in Massachusetts. F.W. swallowed up the last of the city's competing newspapers and moved the *Portsmouth Herald* into the new "Hartford Building" on Congress Street, within sight of the Music Hall entranceway.

His interest in the entertainment business, however, was fading even as movies became the new national pastime. An estimated twenty million Americans were buying a cinema ticket every day, but not to the Portsmouth Theatre on Chestnut Street. Outdated movie projection equipment, talking films, defrayed

ABOVE: *Local bandleader "Bo" Garland took the Music Hall stage with costar Anna Robinson in the Portsmouth DeMolay production of* Bimbo *in 1924. (MHC)*

maintenance, the rise of commercial radio, and the shrinking vaudeville market all took their toll. For the moment, at least, the Olympia and the Colonial ruled over the vintage theater.

The final threat came from the neighboring Franklin Building on Congress Street. Its original Franklin Theatre had been no match for the Music Hall back in 1879 when it opened, nor had the Franklin's experiments with silent movies as early as 1910. Yet in 1924, under new management, the theater inside the massive Franklin Block was reborn as a movie and dance hall popular with sailors and shipyard workers. Renamed the "Arcadia," the opening day crowd of film fans bought 1,342 tickets.

The renovated hall also served as an auditorium for boxing matches and high school basketball games, before focusing on films in 1930. That same year a racy ad for *White Cargo* at the Arcadia Theatre promised an "all talking" movie version of "the play that has made the whole world gasp." The Olympia was offering similar fare with scandal, murder, and divorce in the film *Scarlet Pages*, while the Colonial featured the first talking *Amos 'n' Andy* movie starring two white comedians in blackface makeup.

Downtown in the Depression

"It was an innocent age when I grew up," Winfield Chick recalled to a documentary filmmaker many years ago. Born in 1906, Chick lived around the corner from the Music Hall on Porter Street. As a child he watched crews at the railroad station unloading the "flats" for the traveling vaudeville acts and driving them to the theater by horse and buggy.

"It was magic to us," Chick said, recalling the height of the vaudeville era. "It was another whole world. We didn't see the dirty costumes. We didn't see the holes in the ladies' stockings. We didn't see the old funny makeup. It was all magic."

Eileen Dondero Foley, born to Irish and Italian parents in 1918, grew up above a downtown grocery store and in the city's immigrant North End. She recalled the fading days of live acts, and the friendly competition among cinemas in the 1930s.

OPPOSITE: *(top) This view from the entrance of the Music Hall in the early twentieth century shows the Portsmouth Garage, now demolished, with the surviving Odd Fellows building to the left. (SBM)*

OPPOSITE: *(bottom) Two key characters in the history of the Music Hall are captured in this candid photo outside the Portsmouth Trust & Guarantee Co. around 1910. John Henry Bartlett stands to the left with his son Calvin Page Bartlett whose grandfather, attorney Calvin Page, is to the far right. Bartlett, owner of the Olympia Theatre, was both the son-in-law and law partner of Calvin Page. (ATH)*

Vaudeville shows were becoming a luxury in the hardscrabble days of the Depression.

"There were always five acts," Foley recalled fondly, "and one of them was always an animal show." The best weekend vaudeville played on the Colonial stage, while the Arcadia lured moviegoers with bargain prices and free gifts. Nicknamed "the Scratch House" due to rumors of insect infestation, the Arcadia in the old Franklin Building still managed to fill seats.

"It was always dark," Foley said of the Arcadia. "You never felt good in it. But, on the other hand, the movies were there, and you could stay all afternoon, or all night too." The Arcadia offered free dinnerware to ladies on Tuesdays and Wednesdays. In the 1930s Foley and her friends were drawn in by the promise of special weekly prizes for children.

"I could hardly wait to get there and get one," Foley said of the free gifts, "and it would be something like a buttonhook or something you would never use. Oh, I would get so upset," she laughed. Young Eileen Foley, daughter of Portsmouth's first female mayor, Mary Dondero Foley, grew up to become the longest-serving mayor in the city's history, breaking the record set by F.W. Hartford.

White elephant inherited

Young and old thronged the downtown streets each Saturday during the Great Depression. Money was scarce, but the stores were open, the lights were bright, and the movies were cheap. For the Hartford family, however, the Music Hall had become a heavy burden both financially and emotionally. The aging theater opened only intermittently after 1925. It was used mostly by Portsmouth social groups including DeMolay, the Knights of Columbus, the Elks, and the Garden Club. Minstrel shows, once performed by a hundred blackface professionals, now featured amateur white performers in blackface from St. John's Church, the Portsmouth Naval Shipyard, the Kiwanis Club, and the Boy Scouts of America.

The last best image we have of Fernando W. Hartford shows him standing in an open motorcar, top hat in hand, next to Franklin Delano Roosevelt. The photo is dated July 18, 1932. Roosevelt's car, stopped in the middle of Market Square, is surrounded by a sea of 50,000 onlookers. Hartford was then in his final year as mayor of Portsmouth. Roosevelt was in his final year as governor of New York and a popular Democratic candidate for president of the United States. On the campaign trail during the Depression, Roosevelt promised to deliver a series of programs, public work projects, and reforms known as the "New Deal." The result was a landslide victory for FDR who served an unprecedented four terms as president until his death in 1945.

Economic recovery, however, was slow. The Allied Theatres Company quit leasing the Music Hall in 1933, leaving the once grand structure back in the hands of the Hartford family. Although mostly closed for the next two years, the theater was opened infrequently for dance recitals, high school graduations, and political rallies in the 1930s. As if in memory of the church that once stood on its site, the sleeping hall occasionally woke to the sounds of Jewish, Catholic, and evangelical worship services.

"No man in New Hampshire was better known," the *Manchester Union Leader* reported, following the death of sixty-one-year-old F.W. Hartford in July 1938. Accolades poured in from the *New York Times* and the *Boston Globe*. Fellow editors praised his moral character, nonstop work ethic, engaging personality, and unswerving efforts to promote the city of Portsmouth. One obituary listed over three dozen fraternal, charitable, and civic groups to which Hartford had belonged.

As with the death of Frank Jones, businesses closed and flags stood at half mast for Hartford's funeral at the North Church. "It was a heart-touching scene," the *Herald* reported, when hundreds of mourners "displayed deep feelings as they paid their respects." In true Hartford style the tributes that covered the altar and spilled into the balcony were described as "the most beautiful and extensive floral display ever seen in this section."

"He never inquired as to the nationality or race or creed of anyone in need," Rev. William Safford Jones told the crowded congregation about Hartford. "We are all . . . better citizens, better neighbors, better friends for having known such a man."

These were big shoes to fill. Pulled from his successful military career, Justin Hartford returned to Portsmouth to take over his father's role as newspaper owner and editor even as dark clouds of war spread across Europe and Asia. Just outside his office window loomed another Hartford property. The old theater, empty and bleeding cash, would plague him throughout the coming war until, with no options left, he was forced to put his father's legacy on the auction block. ❧

ABOVE: *Presidential candidate Franklin D. Roosevelt stumps for votes in Market Square on July 18, 1932. Mayor F.W. Hartford, top hat in hand, stands in the backseat of the convertible with the future president. (ATH)*

CHAPTER 6

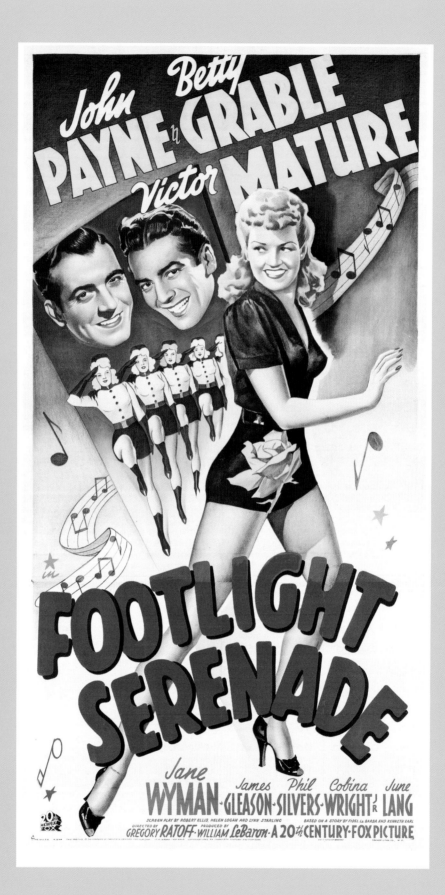

Theater For Sale

From white elephant to Civic cinema

The last thing on Justin Hartford's mind in the 1940s was the shuttered Music Hall he owned just up the hill from his Congress Street newspaper office. Besides taking over his father's stressful job as editor and publisher of the *Portsmouth Herald*, he had a world war to cover. And the city was in a war frenzy. Production at the Portsmouth Naval Shipyard hit a record-breaking pace during World War II as 22,000 employees, men and women, worked three nonstop shifts. From 1941 to 1945 the shipyard produced an unprecedented seventy-nine submarines.

The Music Hall was largely dark, as was much of the city, during forced "blackouts," designed to reduce lights that might be spotted by enemy ships or submarines. Meanwhile, hundreds of soldiers stationed at fortifications along the coast scanned the seas for the enemy attack that never came.

The movie business, however, was in full swing downtown. In 1940 MGM Studios did a survey of all working movie houses on the East Coast. In Portsmouth, the Colonial, Arcadia, and Olympia all received high marks. The slumbering Music Hall, however, was not included in the survey. In January 1942, Justin Hartford reached out to Warner Bros. "circuit management corporation" in hopes of finding someone to take over his aging theater. He was rejected. After inspecting the Music Hall, a Warner Bros. executive wrote to say "this proposition is one which our company cannot handle."

ABOVE: *Founded in 1800, the Portsmouth Naval Shipyard is located in Kittery, Maine, and is currently tasked with the overhaul, repair, and modernization of U.S. Navy submarines. (MIS)*

OPPOSITE: *Renamed the Civic by owner Guy Tott, the upgraded and remodeled Music Hall reopened in 1945 with the movie* Footlight Serenade. *Despite its colorful poster the 1942 musical comedy was filmed in black and white and featured a segment with Betty Grable boxing with her shadow. (MIS)*

As the primary shareholders in Portsmouth Theatre Company, Justin and his mother Lizzie Hartford had to bear the cost of taxes and insurance, more than $2,000 per year, with little or no income. Unable to cash in on the lucrative movie business, early in 1942 Justin received an offer from Charles Fitz, a successful Boston realtor who owned a summer mansion on Rye Beach. Fitz had a serious client, he wrote to Justin, with investors who planned to turn the Music Hall into a nightclub — "which they think might go over big in Portsmouth." But first, they would need a liquor license.

Justin wavered. A hard-knuckle seaport, Portsmouth had been famous for its glitzy, seedy clubs and brothels in the recent past. But Justin's father, F.W. Hartford, had campaigned tirelessly during his tenure to clean up the city's image and bring moral and "high end" professional entertainment to the Music Hall. "I cannot visualize one of the New York or Boston type

BELOW: During World War II workers at the Portsmouth Naval Shipyard broke all records by completing thirty-two submarines in one year including the launch of three submarines on the same day. (ATH)

[nightclubs] doing business in Portsmouth," Justin wrote to Fitz. The deal fizzled.

Unfortunately for the Hartfords, wartime audiences wanted to be distracted and entertained rather than culturally enlightened. Justin's other serious offer that year came from the Boylston Amusement Company in Boston. Again the request for a liquor license came up, and again Justin blinked. He reported that booze was only served in New Hampshire venues that included a "mechanical music machine." In other words, liquor could not be sold during live music performances. Pinball and slot machines — anything that might induce gambling — were also verboten, he pointed out.

"You can drink your beer, eat your food, and listen to the jukebox, but nothing more," Justin wrote to Louis J. Rothenberg, head of the Boylston Amusement Company. Rothenberg, however, was not dissuaded. He made an offer to lease the Music Hall for $2,400 annually, with an option to buy it for $35,000, roughly equal to half a million dollars today. The devil was in the financial details, and the two men continued to squabble by mail for weeks.

The haunting of Mrs. Hartwig

In late spring of 1942, as Justin was grudgingly corresponding with Boylston Amusement, he was approached by a veteran of the "legitimate theater." Maude Hartwig of New York City, owner of the famed Ogunquit Playhouse in nearby Maine, requested a personal tour of the Music Hall. Her husband, Walter Hartwig, had founded the "Little Theater" movement that saw high-quality community playhouses popping up across the country. Their summer repertory theater had begun in an old Ogunquit garage. In 1937 they built the nation's first — and now longest running — seasonal theater. When Walter Hartwig died in 1941, his wife carried on.

Maude instantly fell in love with the abandoned Music Hall. She adored the gilded proscenium arch and the ample backstage built in the Frank Jones era. She imagined creating a year-round performance space in Portsmouth, a city peppered with ancient

ABOVE: *Justin D. Hartford gave up a promising career in the military to take over his father's position as Portsmouth's top newspaper publisher and owner of the deteriorating Music Hall. (ATH)*

mansions and rich in history. Her breathless letter of May 30 to Justin Harford says it all. Mrs. Hartwig wrote:

> What a theater you own and what a thrill it gave me to visit it. The shades of the theater, great with all their pomp and circumstance, passed before my mind's eye — and I saw to the thousands whose burdens were lightened and lives brightened because of those who trod the boards, and gave them all inspiration and showed them Fairyland. To uplift the mind and give a vision is what the theater, the most democratic of the arts, can do best.

"I truly hope," she continued, "that the amusement company of whom you spoke are not permitted to desecrate it. I know that we live in a commercial age, that the Arts, the schools and even the churches are prostituted to the dollar . . . but we do not live by bread alone."

Three days later she wrote again, all but begging to use the Music Hall. "Your theater was haunting me yesterday," she told Justin, who found himself caught in a classic dilemma. While Mrs. Hartwig embodied the quintessential spirit of the performing arts, she was high risk, underfunded, and seeking only a short-term rental for the fall of 1942. Mr. Rothenberg, on the other hand, was all business, and he probably could live by bread alone. So Justin Hartford took the middle road. He leased his theater to the Boylston Amusement Company, and then arranged for Mr. Rothenberg to rent it to Mrs. Hartwig for four months.

But the Portsmouth theater revival was short-lived. Mrs. Hartwig's advance team made a few improvements to the Music Hall stage. Then her New York City-based actors, including many veterans of the Ogunquit Playhouse, delivered four popular plays, including *My Sister Eileen* and a work by Noel Coward. Claire Luce, best known as a stunning blonde dance partner to Fred Astaire, captivated Portsmouth audiences.

LEFT: *A former Ziegfeld Follies dancer, Claire Luce (1903-1989) co-starred in films with Fred Astaire, Humphrey Bogart, and Spencer Tracy. Despite Luce's star power, her appearance in a 1942 play at the Music Hall was a financial failure, ending Maude Hartwig's dream of creating a theater company in Portsmouth. (WIK)*

Attendance, we can assume, was less than hoped for. The show also suffered from the loss of key backstage crewmen who were drafted into the war by Uncle Sam. Even before her lease was up, Mrs. Hartwig and her talented team disappeared.

By December, as Americans felt the impact of wartime food and gasoline rationing, Portsmouth merchants were grumbling to Justin Hartford. Mrs. Hartwig's acting troupe, it seems, had left a variety of unpaid bills in their wake. As the son of a former seven-term mayor, and as editor of the city's only daily newspaper, Justin had a reputation to maintain. "Even though I am not responsible in any way for anything she [Hartwig] has done or not done," Justin wrote to Louis Rothenberg, "you realize that my position in the community is such that I cannot evade even unjust criticism."

There is, however, a happy ending here. Many decades and many owners later, the Music Hall began a holiday collaboration with the now legendary Ogunquit Playhouse. Drawing from top Broadway, television, and film professionals, the Playhouse brought dynamic productions of Disney and Cameron Mackintosh's *Mary Poppins* and Irving Berlin's *White Christmas* to the Portsmouth stage. The creative partnership has since delivered Disney's *Beauty and the Beast*, *Elf the Musical*, and *Annie*, becoming the most popular and the most financially successful series in Music Hall history.

ABOVE: *After Walter Hartwig's death in 1941, wife Maude Hartwig carried on his legacy. She experimented briefly with operating out of the Music Hall in Portsmouth during World War II. We have no clear photograph of Maude. (OPH)*

RIGHT: *Women workers at the Portsmouth Naval Shipyard in World War II. (ATH)*

The final straps

In 1943, as the war intensified, the only memorable event at the old theater was a musical revue featuring singers and dancers of the Portsmouth Harbor Defense team. Among the many U.S. Army soldiers guarding the port and the shipyard, Justin explained to Rothenberg in a letter, were many stage, radio, and movie stars, plus skilled theater technicians. Roughly forty cast and crew had put on a highly professional show each year. Justin hoped, for the good of the war effort, that Boylston Amusement would allow the talented military men to use the Music Hall for free. They did. The Harbor Defense show, entitled *Keep Mum, Chum* was especially poignant for the submarine-building families of Portsmouth who truly understood that, in times of war, "loose lips sink ships."

The two businessmen never got along. Within a year Justin was threatening Rothenberg — who also ran the neighboring Arcadia Theater and at least ten other regional cinemas — with a lawsuit. Boylston Amusement was already in arrears for $3,295 of unpaid insurance fees, taxes, and lease payments on the Music Hall. Rothenberg's company, Justin complained to his lawyer, had also wrecked a boiler and removed toilet fixtures from his theater. When the lawyer attempted to schedule a face-to-face meeting, both men claimed to be too sick to attend.

Acting groups continued to inquire about putting on shows and were routinely turned down. In October 1943 Justin explained his position once more to Austin Fairman, a British-born actor who hoped to rent the facility. The Music Hall, Justin wrote to Fairman, was simply a building, available to anyone who had "the background and the wherewithal to operate it." He stressed that, "The Portsmouth Theatre Company is not made up of theatrical people or of anyone who has had any experience in show business." The Hartfords simply owned the building.

Fairman, who had recently appeared in the film *British Intelligence* (1940) with Boris Karloff, tried to impress Justin with his credentials. Fairman promised to employ only "thoroughly competent Actors [with a capital "A"], not the "summer theatre variety!" There would be high-class New York shows, Fairman promised, interspersed with "big-time vaudeville" acts and

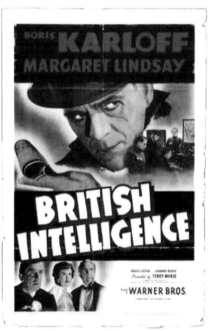

ABOVE: *World War II-era posters for* Keep Mum Chum *and for* British Intelligence, *a film featuring British actor Austin Fairman who made a failed attempt to establish an acting company at the Music Hall. (MIS)*

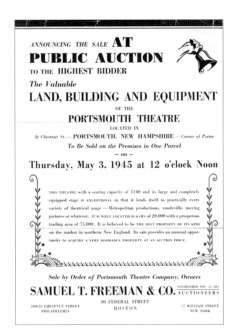

classy Sunday concerts. His goal, Fairman wrote, was to create "a permanent acting company for Portsmouth" with the Music Hall as his base of operations.

Justin had heard it all before, but he tentatively agreed to a six-month lease. "It is all a gamble, of course, with them," Justin's realtor warned him, "and I suppose you might only get one month's rent."

The realtor was right. After many bold promises, the newly formed Fairman Players presented a former Broadway comedy entitled *Separate Rooms*. An undated handwritten note soon appeared at the front desk of the *Portsmouth Herald* offices next door. The note read: "This is to inform you that we find it impossible to continue at the Portsmouth Theatre and hereby enclose [the] key to same and forfeit the money placed on deposit against rent. It is discouraging to say the least, but we have left your property much improved and that is a little consolation for us."

Offers from hopeful but impoverished actors continued to trickle in during 1944 and early 1945. All were politely turned down. A developer, claiming to be an old friend of Mayor F.W. Hartford, suggested converting the theater into a bowling alley. Another "serious" buyer from New York abruptly pulled out of a lease negotiation. New film projectors, he informed Justin, were unavailable due to the war, and old projectors were too costly. Enough was enough. The Music Hall had to go.

Gone in twenty minutes

As Japan and Germany teetered on the edge of defeat in World War II, and as America mourned the death of President Franklin Delano Roosevelt, the shareholders of the Portsmouth Theatre Company called it quits. Justin and his mother Lizzie asked Samuel T. Freedman, a Boston auctioneer, to dispose of their failing investment as quickly as possible. The Music Hall, according to a well-illustrated promotional brochure, "is believed to be the best property of its kind on the market in northern New England." The historic parcel of downtown land, site of an early almshouse, prison, and church, went on the auction block.

ABOVE: *A detail from the auction brochure advertising the sale of the Music Hall in 1945. Guy Tott of Kittery, Maine, purchased the rundown 1878 theater for a mere $10,000. (JDR)*

The sale included the 1878 Peirce family building, the addition created by Frank Jones, and all the equipment in the theater.

The auction, held at noon on May 3, 1945, was over almost the moment it began. Although an estimated fifty people attended the sale, including potential big city theater owners, the first bid was a pitiful $5,000. That bid was quickly rejected. The next was submitted by Guy Tott, a former shipyard electrician and contractor from nearby Kittery, Maine. Tott doubled the offer to $10,000, a far cry from the theater's assessed value of $35,000. But with no other bidders, Mr. Tott's offer was accepted. In twenty minutes the Hartford dynasty, begun in 1903, was over. So was the war.

"I have no definite plans at the moment," Guy Tott told the *Portsmouth Herald* immediately following the auction. But he promised to reveal his plans after making "two important phone calls." A brief newspaper notice of the Music Hall sale was upstaged by a bold front page headline announcing the death of Adolf Hitler due to an apparent suicide. The very next day, May 4, Germany surrendered.

On May 15 Guy Tott introduced his new manager, Herman Smith, who said extensive renovations were about to begin. The restored theater, Smith told the press, would be renamed the "Civic." That bit of news, too, was overshadowed by the "unbounded excitement" that gripped the city the same day.

ABOVE: *Photographs from the 1945 Music Hall auction brochure. (MHC)*

The first of four Nazi U-boats, captured in the North Atlantic sea, was being towed into Portsmouth Harbor. Locals rushed to catch a glimpse of the defeated German submariners. Over the summer, as work on the former Music Hall continued, on orders from President Harry Truman, the United States dropped atomic bombs on the Japanese cities of Hiroshima and Nagasaki. In September 1945, Japan surrendered. Days later the Civic opened.

On September 29, 1945, Justin sent a letter to his former partner. "Dear Mother," he wrote, "The business concerning the dissolution of the Portsmouth Theatre Company has finally been completed." A few minor stockholders were being paid off, he wrote, and as the key owner of ninety-six shares, Lizzie Hartford was due $5,688.80. Because the liquidated stock had devalued from the days of F.W. Hartford, Lizzie was also entitled to a tax loss of $4,868.70. The letter, with a sizable check enclosed, was signed "as always, J.D. Hartford, Treasurer."

Almost lost to history, the newest owner should rank among the saviors of the city's oldest theater. Beyond the usual scrubbing, repainting, and polishing, Guy Tott's team installed a modern telephone system, professional stage lighting, and a new marquee. Tott replaced 1,200 wooden seats with 900 cushioned metal seats and exchanged the worn movie screen with the biggest indoor screen in town. The addition of two top

RIGHT: *For the next forty years the Music Hall would become a movie house known as the Civic. (ATH)*

quality carbon arc film projectors made by the Brenkert Light Projection Co. of Detroit transformed the Civic into the city's most attractive and state-of-the-art cinema.

The widely promoted opening weekend featured Betty Grable in the film musical *Footlight Serenade*. The audience applauded as Portsmouth's first female mayor, Mary Dondero, and her daughter Eileen took their place in the elaborately decorated box seats. "I felt like a queen on a throne," Eileen Foley recalled. Forty years later, then mayor of the city herself, she attended the re-opening of the Music Hall once more.

With his theater fully outfitted to show movies, Guy Tott also tried to bring back vaudeville. A surviving Civic poster from November 1945 offers a "Big Vodvil Show" starring the goats, ponies, monkeys, and dogs of Capt. Anderson's Circus. Ted Wright's five-piece orchestra performed between seven live acts. The evening concluded with a screening of the latest Hollywood gangster film, *Dillinger*, billed as "the most feared and wanton gunman since Jesse James." A loyal booster of the Navy, Guy Tott gave shipyard workers and sailors 800 free tickets to the show that same weekend to honor the arrival of the USS *Portsmouth*. He also agreed to send one vaudeville act each week to entertain the inmates at the Portsmouth Naval Prison, the hulking white concrete castle on the Piscataqua River.

LEFT: *Early Civic projectionist Barry Fritz on the job courtesy of Sarah Lachance and Trevor Bartlett. (MIS)*

ABOVE: *A screening of the controversial anti-drug film* Reefer Madness *briefly closed the Civic in 1947. The following year the nearby Colonial Theatre premiered the American "race film"* Lost Boundaries *by local producer Louis de Rochemont, best known for his* The March of Time *newsreel series. (JDR)*

Loew and behold

The refurbished Civic was hot stuff. The sparkling new concession stand on the second floor offered ice cream sundaes, cold sodas, and fresh popcorn. Young usherettes in blue uniforms waving flashlights guided patrons to their comfortable seats. Portsmouth's competing cinemas were less than pleased by the Rip Van Winkle-like return of the old theater after its twenty year nap. Owner Guy Tott and a succession of managers found themselves in a heady competition for first-run movies with the Colonial, Olympia, and Arcadia, then owned by Paramount pictures. Consumers were the big winners as downtown movie houses lured them in with another round of free dishware, door prizes, deep discounts, and special community events.

In May of 1947 local narcotics agents briefly shut down the Civic for showing the film *Reefer Madness*. Originally funded by a religious group, the poorly-acted melodrama was first released in 1936. But what began as a propaganda film decrying the evils of marijuana turned into a cult classic when another producer inserted "salacious and exploitative" scenes not found in the original. In 1948, a year after the *Reefer Madness* scandal at the Civic, the *Portsmouth Herald* reprinted a national news piece headlined "Reefer Smoking on Increase in U.S." The addictive weed, according to the article, was known to users as "Mary Warner" and "has the greatest appeal to people of addictive personality."

On June 22, 1949, all eyes were on the Colonial and Olympia theaters. That's when local filmmaker Louis de Rochemont, best known for his *The March of Time* newsreels, introduced *Lost Boundaries*, a film about an African-American family "passing" as white. It was, for the times, a rare "race" film, shot largely in the seacoast area and included many black cast members. It was Portsmouth's first "world premier" and it drew 3,100 viewers to four showings at the two downtown cinemas. The *Portsmouth Herald* reported the audience had to "choke back the emotions aroused by the bold story."

Exactly when Guy Tott began an alliance with Elias Moishe Loew is unclear, but it was likely soon after the Civic opened. Despite the best of intentions, the Kittery entrepreneur lacked the clout to take on the powerful Paramount theater franchise. E.M. Loew, a Boston-based company named for its owner, would eventually operate hotels, motels, a racetrack, a nightclub, and seventy theaters with another seventeen drive-ins.

Born in 1897 in what is currently Ukraine, Elias M. Loew arrived in the United States around age thirteen as a penniless immigrant. After working as a watchmaker's apprentice and as a breadboy at a restaurant, Loew borrowed enough money to revive an old movie theater in Lynn, Massachusetts. In 1947 the New England theater magnate leased the Civic from Guy Tott and became a one-third owner. By this time Loew and his then-wife Sonja, a "Czechoslovakian beauty," were well known for their opulent lifestyle.

The following year newspapers breathlessly reported that Mrs. Loew, now divorced from her wealthy husband, had been robbed of $50,000 in jewelry. Thieves left Sonja bound and gagged "with twelve new pairs of nylon stockings" in the bathroom of her fifth-floor, New York City hotel suite. Mrs. Loew was unharmed and the thieves were quickly captured.

Elias Loew was not, as many have assumed, related to the wealthy Marcus Loew, who merged three Hollywood studios to create Metro-Goldwyn-Mayer. But Elias Loew was influential enough, thanks to his chain of New England cinemas, to pull in the first-run films that the Civic desperately needed for success.

Guy Tott died in 1948 at age fifty-six. The *Herald* reported that his estate, valued at $15,000, passed to his widow. Marie Tott and her two adult daughters retained partial ownership of the Civic for many years, but it was Elias Loew who ran the show. Loew's efforts to give Portsmouth audiences the most for their money paid off. By the early 1950s both the Arcadia and the Olympia were closed and eventually converted to office space. When, years later, Paramount elected to sell off the Colonial, Elias Loew grabbed up the Market Square movie house and renamed it the "Cinema."

ABOVE: *News photos of theater mogul Elias M. Loew (1897-1984) and his first wife Sonja. In this publicity shot Mrs. Loew is holding the nylon stockings used to bind and gag her during a robbery. (JDR)*

Our Mr. Brooks

As Frank Jones knew well, the best asset a business owner can have is a good manager. That goes double for the theater biz where the manager must oversee film schedules, ticket sales, snack bar supplies, rentals, live acts, finances, staff training, building maintenance, and publicity — all while keeping hundreds of daily audience members happy. For Elias Loew, that man in Portsmouth was Walter Brooks, a burly, kindly, bespectacled, crew-cut man in a dark suit. Brooks arrived at Portsmouth from Worcester in the early 1950s and stayed with the Civic until it closed more than thirty years later.

Brooks witnessed the dying days of vaudeville in the old theater. The last big New York City acts, he recalled in an interview, were so embarrassed to perform at the Civic that they insisted on using false names. One man who roller skated on stage wearing a straitjacket insisted his act was unique. When Walter Brooks pointed out that he had featured an identical act the previous week, the performer threatened to sue. The final blow to live acts in Portsmouth, Brooks recalled, was a nearly sold-out performance of the opera *Carmen*. When the opera company failed to show up, he had to refund the entire audience. "After *Carmen*," Brooks told a Music Hall historian, "the people that owned the theater said — you know, let's just stick to acts that come in a [film] can."

The end of vaudeville in the Fifties ushered in a brief golden era of film at the Civic. Malls, multiplexes, and drive-in theaters had not yet arrived. Early television was fuzzy, uptight, and black and white. Repeat customers, Brooks recalled, patronized the big screen movies at least once or twice each week. There was the occasional theater burglary, according to the newspaper, and an attack by a rowdy patron caught carving his initials in the balcony wall. But business at the Civic was brisk enough to force Paramount to close the Arcadia and the Olympia.

The decline of the Civic, too, was only a matter of time. The old theater needed constant repair, Brooks noted, and customer parking was a perennial issue. Heating the enormous space cost up to $1,400 per week in winter. Big film distributors, Brooks explained, quickly lost interest in downtown single-screen

ABOVE: *A young Walter Brooks who managed the Civic and Cinema theaters in downtown Portsmouth over four decades. (WBF)*

ABOVE: *The former Colonial Theatre in Market Square was converted to the Cinema as part of the E.M. Loew chain of movie houses and managed by Walter Brooks (inset). Closed in the mid-1980s, the theater lobby was converted into a record shop, but the entire building was later demolished. (ATH)*

venues. Worse yet, managers were required to bid on first run films sight unseen, with no advance screenings. Instead of introducing a new film every three or four days, managers were pressured to contract films for weeks, even if they bombed at the box office.

"That would be like you're buying a dress or a pair of shoes without seeing what they look like," Brooks said. "And it became unprofitable."

Film expert Trevor Bartlett, the "quintessential latchkey kid," recalls sheltering in the Civic with friends on hot or rainy summer days when he was nine or ten. Mr. Brooks sold the boys their seventy-five-cent tickets. The manager climbed to the second floor and manned the popcorn machine, then hauled himself up the stairs to the balcony where he lit the two antique carbon arc projectors, as big as battleships, and screened the film. There were usually no more than twenty people in the audience, Bartlett, says, and he came to feel the Civic was his own personal sanctuary and portal to adventure.

"It was a faded, dim, cavernous, moldering husk of a building in decline," Bartlett reminisces. "The dome was cracked, the paint was chipped, the columns and proscenium were disintegrating. I remember one time watching, under the flickering light of the movie screen above, a rat the size of a raccoon humping its way across the stage. We hucked some Milk Duds at the beast, but it just ignored us."

ABOVE: *A candid photo on Chestnut Street from the Civic premiere of* The Love Bug *(1968), a Walt Disney live action comedy starring a Volkswagen Beetle named Herbie.* (WBF)

OPPOSITE: *(top) The nadir of Civic fare was arguably* Mark of the Devil, *a shocking film rated "V" for violence and promoted with the distribution of free vomit bags for viewers.* (MIS)

OPPOSITE: *(bottom) A high point at the Cinema, meanwhile, was the glitzy Hollywood premiere of the 1959 adventure flick* John Paul Jones. *The real John Paul Jones had rented rooms during the Revolutionary War in a house only a few yards from the modern day Music Hall.* (JDR)

And then there were two

Unknown to most, the Colonial Theater in Market Square was teetering on the edge of insolvency in 1959 when it hosted the world premiere of the Warner Brothers epic film *John Paul Jones*. Actor Robert Stack, who played the swashbuckling naval hero, did not attend the event, nor did co-stars Bette Davis, Peter Cushing, or Marisa Pavan. But there was plenty of glitz and enough minor dignitaries to please the Portsmouth audience. During the American Revolution the real Captain Jones, a Scot by birth, had boarded in a Portsmouth home while outfitting his warships. Now a museum, the John Paul Jones House still stands just a few yards from the Music Hall's backstage doors.

In 1963 Paramount sold the Colonial, its last Portsmouth theater, to E.M. Loew. Assigned to manage both Loew movie houses, Walter Brooks elected to keep his office at the Civic. The following year a fire devastated the block adjacent to the Colonial in Market Square. The theater survived, but suffered significant smoke damage. Curiously, the fire led to a complete makeover of the Colonial that, in turn, sent the Civic into a slow and deadly decline.

After months of work totaling $200,000, the restored Colonial — renamed the "Cinema" — opened in February 1966. The Cinema boasted a new screen, plush seats, and wall-to-wall carpeting. Loew's company renovated the restrooms, floors, box office, and concession stand. Loew added "flameless electric heat" and, best of all, air conditioning. The smelly, smoky seats from the former Colonial were moved to the balcony of the Civic, now relegated mostly to second-run and B-movies. An army veteran with a degree in business, manager Brooks soldiered on for the eccentric Elias Loew who was, he reported, "always a good boss." As a full-on movie geek, Brooks employed his vast knowledge of films in every genre to keep both theaters hovering in the black.

The exact day the Civic hit bottom is debatable. Many locals will recall (but few will admit attending) the theater's intermittent flirtation with X-rated fare. The trailer for the erotic *Emmanuelle* (1974) whispered seductively, "Lets you feel good, without feeling bad." But there was no denying the unabashed

THEATRE PHOTOGRAPH and REPORT

State: _____ N. H. _____ City: _____ PORTSMOUTH _____

Branch: _____ BOSTON _____ Zone: _____

Date Photo Taken: _____ 5/41 _____ Theatre Name: _____ ARCADIA _____

Street Address: _____ MAIN ST. _____
City Population (1940): _____ 14, _____
Competing Theatres: _____ COLONIAL _____

Is Theatre an M-G-M Customer Now? _____ NO _____
How Long Has It Been Playing M-G-M Product? _____
Date Built: _____ 1925 _____ Condition: _____ POOR _____
Seats: Main Floor _____ 500 _____ Balcony _____ 300 _____
Type of Patronage: _____ CITY — NAVY YARD _____

Balcony for Colored?

Signed: _____ [signature] _____ Branch Manager

ABOVE: During a 1940 survey of American movie houses, a researcher from MGM Studios documented the condition of three downtown Portsmouth cinemas. This is the rating card for the Arcadia on Congress Street. (ATH)

adult content of films like *Intimate Playmates* and *The Swingin' Stewardesses* (1976). Then came *Mark of the Devil*, a German-made schlockfest billed as "Positively the most terrifying film ever made." Set in Austria and rated "V for violence," this exploitation film graphically depicted the torture of women accused of witchcraft. It was marketed in the United States by the distribution of vomit bags. Printed in blood red ink, each souvenir barf bag read, "Guaranteed to upset your stomach." As the carnage played out on screen, a live bat buzzed the audience in the balcony.

Brooks manned both forts in what was ultimately a losing battle. Color cable television and home video recorders were wiping out grand old theaters from coast to coast. New multi-screen shoebox theaters, each identical to the next, were popping up across New England in the early 1970s. Brooks also had to compete with seasonal drive-ins at nearby Kittery, North Hampton, and Newington. As shoppers moved to the malls with acres of free parking, many downtown Portsmouth stores stood empty.

"I always had an idea of making three theaters out of [the Civic] with two in the front," Brooks later reminisced. "You'd walk up an aisle and have a third one backstage, upstairs. But I never wanted to touch the architectural look."

To fill seats, Brooks delivered massive discounts and an extraordinary range of movies. The winners this time were a new generation of film fanatics who grew up watching art house and vintage flicks, Disney classics, spy thrillers, rock operas, adventure, western, horror, science fiction, and monster movies.

"The Civic was our home away from home when we were kids," one regular customer recalls, and he effortlessly lists dozens of movie titles he attended. Parents dumped off carloads of children who paid ninety-nine cents for an afternoon double-feature — ten cents more to sit in the balcony and raise hell. "It was the only affordable theater in the area," another patron

remembers. While still in middle school, he somehow gained entrance to R-rated comedies like *Caddyshack* (1980) and *Animal House* (1978).

The one-hundredth anniversary of the Music Hall passed without notice in 1978. Despite frequent customer sightings, Walter Brooks laughed off rumors that the old playhouse was haunted. He refused a request from would-be ghostbusters to set up their "crazy" paranormal recording machines. Decades of gum-chewing, candy-throwing, Coke-spilling patrons, however, had left something palpable and gooey behind. Locals who knew the Civic well still refer to it reverently as "Old Stickyfoot." But for theater-mogul Elias M. Loew, like Justin Hartford before him, this hallowed hall was ultimately a chunk of real estate. And by the early 1980s, it was once again time for the owner to cash out. ❧

ABOVE: *Photos of the Olympia and Colonial (later the Cinema) as seen in the MGM survey of 1940. The Music Hall, then largely closed and out of date, was not considered a viable venue for MGM films and was not included in the survey. (ATH)*

CHAPTER 7

The Portsmouth Renaissance

Rebooting the "Old Town by the Sea"

Let's press rewind. To understand how a dilapidated Victorian Music Hall became what the *Boston Globe* later called "the beating heart" of twenty-first-century Portsmouth, we need to circle back to 1964. That's when a pair of local high school teachers, Sally and Stanley Flowers, gambled $2,500 of their own savings to launch Theatre by the Sea.

The tiny but professional repertory company settled into the bottom of a towering brick building across from a row of tugboats on Ceres Street in the city's North End. The former grain warehouse once opened directly onto the busy wharves where tall ships from around the globe unloaded their goods. Volunteers transformed the dank rat-infested basement into an intimate performance space only five rows deep. Portsmouth's first theater in 1790 had opened and quickly closed on Bow Street only yards away.

Word of Theatre by the Sea spread quickly. Curious audience members from as far away as Boston came to check out the funky, handmade, sometimes leaky, 108-seat playhouse. According to one early reviewer, Portsmouth was still a "time-worn undistinguished town." Ceres Street, little more than a waterfront back alley, was considered the "risky" part of town better known for

ABOVE: *Young Theatre by the Sea actors double as maintenance crew on Ceres Street. (ATH)*

OPPOSITE: *View of the tugboats off Ceres Street in the 1960s, site of the old ferry that took passengers across the fast-flowing Piscataqua River to Maine. The arrival of Theatre by the Sea and a small cluster of unique restaurants and shops here — combined with the opening of Strawbery Banke Museum in the South End — launched the city's cultural and economic revival. The distant steeple in this photo by Douglas Armsden is St. John's Episcopal Church. (ATH)*

RIGHT: *Cast of the play* Pippin *at Theatre by the Sea. Actor Scott Weintraub is in the center in black.* (WIN)

its topless bars. But no one could deny that the TBS actors were top-notch while the plays were daring and sophisticated.

America was a very different place in 1964, the year the Beatles first appeared on the *Ed Sullivan Show*. It was the year the Boston Strangler killed his thirteenth victim and Cassius Clay beat the world heavyweight boxing champion Sonny Liston. Even as he escalated an unwinnable war in Vietnam, President Lyndon Johnson made history by signing the Civil Rights Act that ended segregation in public places and banned employers from discriminating on the basis of race, color, religion, sex, or national origin. The times, as folk singer Bob Dylan proclaimed, were a-changin'.

The deaths of 109 crewmen lost aboard the sunken submarine USS *Thresher* in 1963 still haunted the city. And there were rumors that the entire Portsmouth Naval Shipyard might be closed by federal decree. The new Pease Air Force Base, meanwhile, having swallowed up 3,578 acres of land by eminent

ABOVE: *Within its first few years Theatre by the Sea on Ceres Street set a high bar by mixing traditional fare like* Twelfth Night *and* The Glass Menagerie *with newer works including* The Fantasticks, K2, *and* Who's Afraid of Virginia Woolf? *The carved sign over the door is now in the collection of the Portsmouth Athenaeum. (ATH)*

ABOVE: *Created by untrained chef James "Buddy" Haller, the Blue Strawbery on Ceres Street kick-started the trend of inventive cuisine that thrives in Portsmouth today. A pioneer in the yet-to-be-named local food movement, Haller became known for creating recipes out of what was available. (HAL)*

domain, had swelled the city's population to a record 26,900. Bombers and jets roared overhead en route to a distant war.

It was a tough time to promote fine arts in a blue collar military port. The average American earned $6,000 in 1964 and the average house sold for just $13,050. Despite critical raves, by 1965 Theatre by the Sea was near financial collapse. TBS actors, who doubled as the maintenance crew, were paid only $50 per long exhausting week, less than a dollar an hour. By the end of its first season the nascent company needed $50,000 to stay open for another year. One supporter, writing to the *Portsmouth Herald*, claimed that closing TBS would be "a smear on the reputation of Portsmouth" and would prove "we are a narrow, tight, small-minded group of people." Benefactors got the message. Within months the theater was back on its feet.

Residents often note (with more nostalgia than fact) that few dared walk down Ceres Street until the arrival of TBS. Branded as the city's "Olde Harbour" area in the late 1960s, the Ceres and Bow Street section soon caught on. "Once decayed and wino-haunted," the *Boston Globe* reported, the waterfront alley had become "chic and fashionable." The metamorphosis was complete, travel writers reported, with the arrival of the Blue Strawbery in 1970. Founder James "Buddy" Haller opened his tiny gourmet restaurant in another brick warehouse a few paces down Ceres Street. Haller's funky-yet-sophisticated menu was the perfect complement to an evening at Theatre by the Sea. Classy eateries like the Dolphin Striker and the Oar House sprang up nearby amid a cluster of unique new shops including Salamandra Glass, the Trunk Shop, and Macro Polo. An alluring new destination was born and people from elsewhere took notice.

"In my opinion," Dolphin Striker owner Peter Rice later told the *NH Times*, "there is no question that the restaurants, above any other single group, started the business renaissance of downtown Portsmouth."

The cultural revival on the North End waterfront, according to Peter Rice, was sparked by developer Richard Morton who invested heavily in the string of nineteenth-century brick buildings he owned. Morton also supported the theater, shops, offices, and restaurants that moved into his buildings. That revival was matched in the South End by the opening of Strawbery Banke Museum, a ten-acre campus of historic buildings.

According to legend, local librarian Dorothy Vaughan had sparked the city's biggest preservation project in 1957 when she nervously addressed the all-male Portsmouth Rotary Club. If they continued to tear down the city's historic buildings, she warned, Portsmouth was doomed to become "Anywhere, USA." Vaughan was, in fact, only one of a series of influential preservationists who spoke to local businessmen. These national experts promised that saving and restoring Portsmouth's architectural treasures would attract tourist dollars and help revive the city's flagging downtown economy.

ABOVE: *The iconic Blue Strawbery Restaurant poster. (HAL)*

Tapping into federal funds, Portsmouth transformed the "blighted" low-income Puddle Dock neighborhood from a preservation project into what has become a family-friendly museum. Strawbery Banke encompasses thirty-seven historic buildings dating from 1695 to the mid-1800s. "Portsmouth Slum Clearance Marks New Era" the *Christian Science Monitor* reported in the 1960s. But for long-time residents of the close-knit neighborhood, the revival was more like an enemy invasion. Over a hundred families were displaced to create the nonprofit museum. Uprooted by urban renewal and rising property taxes, many natives were embittered by the gentrification and tsunami of tourism that followed.

By the time Strawbery Banke Museum opened in 1965, the year following Theatre by the Sea, there was no stopping what the media dubbed the "Renaissance" of Portsmouth. Although only a few of its buildings were initially restored, by 1971 Strawbery Banke was attracting 30,000 visitors annually. That number has since tripled. The alluring blend of history, arts, and fine dining made the old seaport a popular stop for day-trippers. Vacationers heading to Maine began to exit the Interstate to see if the buzz about Portsmouth was real. Massachusetts residents who routinely stocked up on liquor, lottery tickets, and cigarettes at the "no tax" New Hampshire traffic circle also began to check out the historic downtown.

Trading on Portsmouth's rising reputation as a destination for day-trippers, locals created more reasons to visit. To celebrate the redesigned "tourist friendly" city center, for example, Pro Portsmouth created Market Square Day, an annual street festival that drew thousands to the beautified downtown. Theatre by the Sea staged musicals to thousands more each night under the stars at the Prescott Park Arts Festival. TBS was soon joined by a cluster of even smaller theater groups, two mime troupes, a ballet company, and a jazz and dance ensemble. Tall ships, courted by local businessmen, sailed once more into port. Thanks to the Press Room, the Rusty Hammer, Rosa's, the Ferry Landing, Clarence's Chowder House, Ceres Bakery and more, the media branded Portsmouth "The Restaurant Capital of the Northeast." Dance clubs sprouted across town and music of every style filled the salt air.

ABOVE: *Market Square Day, seen here from the roof of the Portsmouth Athenaeum, is an annual celebration of the city's cultural renaissance and the revival of the downtown area in the late 1970s and early '80s. (JDR)*

"I know of no other place in the country," musician Harvey Reid wrote in a weekly arts publication called *re:Ports*, "where there is so much good live music per capita." The tiny town, one reporter noted, now offered a "bewildering string of bars and nightclubs."

By 1981, according to the *NH Times*, Portsmouth had evolved from "a dingy little seacoast enclave" into "the most exciting town in New Hampshire." Dorothy Vaughan, never at a loss for a pithy quote, told *U.S. News & World Report*, "We've hit rock bottom. We're coming up."

ABOVE: *An early logo for Strawbery Banke Museum. (SBM)*

ABOVE: *(left) Founded in 1958 to preserve a ten-acre neighborhood of historic South End homes, Strawbery Banke Museum opened in 1965. It has since become one of New England's favorite historic destinations. The Goodwin Mansion, seen here, is one of more than thirty buildings on campus. (SBM)*

"A bit of a backwater for more than a century," the *Boston Globe* proclaimed, "Portsmouth has had a renaissance in recent years, rediscovering itself and changing from an oversized museum town into a lively year-round city."

Facing financial facts

ABOVE: *Among the beloved affordable eateries of the period was Clarence's Chowder House on Market Street, a funky laid-back hangout featuring live folk music run by chef Mary Jane Moulton. (MIS)*

Ironically, it was during the flowering of the Portsmouth Renaissance that the Civic movie house, formerly the Music Hall, withered and died. The proliferation of malls, cable television, and video players convinced movie theater mogul Elias M. Loew that it was time to get rid of his two downtown buildings. Three days before Christmas in 1982 the new owner, with the unremarkable name of Exchange Title Holders, bought and sold the buildings within a day. The next owner was Continental Properties, LLC of California.

Walter Brooks, who had managed the Civic and the Cinema for three decades, kept up appearances for a while before departing for movie houses in Hampton and Dover. Rumors flew. The aging Portsmouth cinemas would soon be flattened for parking lots, locals whispered, or gutted for condominiums. Some said the Civic was fated to become a seminar center for a computer company.

"No comment," an executive for the new owners told the *Rockingham Gazette* in 1982. "I'm really not at liberty to

ABOVE: *Portsmouth's cultural renaissance was also driven by many talented and independent musicians, dancers, artists, writers, and other performers, many still active today, including the nonprofit Kitchensink Mime Theatre (now NH Theatre Project) (top), Pontine Movement Theatre (left), and Generic Theatre (bottom). (NHT/PON/GEN)*

speculate," he grumbled. "I really wish people would wait until we tell them. It's all idle speculation."

Theatre by the Sea, too, was inching its way onto the endangered list. Thanks to loyal benefactors, TBS had moved in the late 1970s to a larger 263-seat facility in a renovated old brick brewery on Bow Street. But the brave little group that had kicked off the Portsmouth cultural revival was becoming a victim of its own success. Plagued by money problems and a million dollar annual budget, facing management turmoil, and competing against a host of local performers — something had to go. A spokesperson announced on April 1, 1983, that TBS could no longer offer summer musicals at Prescott Park. The entire seacoast let out a collective wail of disappointment.

Actor Scott Weintraub, his wife Nancy, and a dedicated team of talented volunteers jumped in to salvage the festival. When the Weintraubs headed to Los Angeles after two summers, the newly formed Prescott Park Arts Festival Inc. took over. This highly successful, sometimes controversial, nonprofit agency has kept the beloved waterfront summer performance series alive ever since. But it was curtains for Theatre by the Sea. After more than two decades, TBS would be replaced by Portsmouth Academy of Performing Arts (PAPA) and its performance company Seacoast Repertory Theatre that currently operates on Bow Street year round.

Keeping so many creative and historical nonprofits going in such a small city was becoming a problem. An influx of major corporations, attracted to the enhanced quality of life along the seacoast, was helpful. Companies including Data General, Liberty Mutual, Signal Capital, and Congoleum stepped up as nonprofit benefactors. But the public was slow to underwrite the cultural revolution.

In the summer of 1983 students from the nearby University of New Hampshire conducted a survey. While institutions like Strawbery Banke Museum had achieved ninety-nine percent name recognition among residents, the student poll concluded, only five percent of seacoast homes were dues-paying members of a local arts or history organization. Was the recent economic recession to blame, or poor marketing, or apathy?

David Choate III, president of the Greater Portsmouth Chamber of Commerce, said that, in order to survive, creative nonprofits needed to think and operate more like businesses. According to the UNH survey, a growing number of arts and history groups were financially dependent on "a tiny little constituency" of seacoast residents. The bulk of nonprofit support was coming from "people from outside the area." In other words, Portsmouth's rising economy was tied to summer tourists, the same tourists, many locals complained, who were clogging the city's streets, sidewalks, and parking spaces. "Can they deal with the truth? I don't know," Choate said of the struggling arts and history nonprofits.

By the mid-1980s the two-decades-long Portsmouth Renaissance had drawn a small army of creative young women and men to the heart of the city where rents were, for the moment, still affordable. What had begun as a series of disconnected experiments in promoting local arts and culture was beginning to look like a movement. The idea that Portsmouth was in the midst of a cultural rebirth was a source of pride for many, as well as a source of income for others. "Portsmouth today is a magnet for people and money," one newspaper reported.

There were growing pains, of course, including a rise in the crime rate, political squabbles, a drain on city resources, and the inevitable leap in property taxes that pushed up rents. Battle lines

ABOVE: *The ever-popular waterfront gardens at Prescott Park in the city's historic South End. (JDR)*

developed. Those who favored turning Portsmouth into a tourist mecca faced off against the "old guard" who resisted the changes.

Portsmouth's "identity crisis" found its way onto the cover of the *Boston Globe Magazine.* Evelyn Marconi, a South Ender whose home had been razed during the creation of Strawbery Banke Museum, pulled no punches. "The revitalization of Portsmouth was a big flop," Marconi told the magazine. "Plastic City, USA. All revitalized downtowns look the same."

But there was no holding back the tide of change. As big New Hampshire cities like Manchester, Concord, and Nashua looked on, the media continued to focus on Portsmouth's "growing reputation as a little town with urbane ways." No amount of public wrangling, another newspaper suggested, could slow down "a centuries old city that has endured infernos, and embargoes, and Indian attacks."

The economic impact of Pease Air Force Base and the Portsmouth Naval Shipyard was giving way to income from tourism and the arrival of high-tech corporations. Portsmouth now had a new hospital, a Children's Museum, a replica sailing ship known as a "gundalow," a submarine museum, and a downtown Sheraton Hotel. Topless bars had been replaced by tapas restaurants. The arrival of the sprawling 676,500 square foot Fox Run Mall in nearby Newington, which many feared would kill business in Portsmouth, only seemed to stimulate downtown merchants to up their game. "Sometimes it takes a real kick in the ass to get people moving," Chamber president David Choate told the *Globe.*

Music Hall reborn

The natives were restless. Charles Cook, spokesperson for the latest owner of the Civic and the Cinema, tried to calm worried movie lovers. Late in the fall of 1984, Cook promised he would keep the doors open throughout the coming holiday season by screening a series of low-cost art films. "It's somewhat of a risk," he told the media, "but I'm willing to take the chance." Locals turned out in droves to support the last picture shows, but to no avail. Costly winter heating bills were too much for the cavernous

ABOVE: *The flat-bottomed gundalow was once a key mode of transporting goods throughout the rivers and bays of the Piscataqua region. The creation of the replica gundalow* Capt. Edward H. Adams *in 1982 inspired the twenty-first century construction of the gundalow* Piscataqua, *seen here on its maiden voyage, that can carry passengers. (GUN)*

structures. As a new year dawned, the Civic and its sister Cinema were shuttered once more.

The future of the Civic, as described by theater historians Zhana Morris and Trevor Bartlett, was bleak. "Long years of hot summers, hard rains, and harsh winters had exacted a terrible toll on the neglected old structure," they wrote. "Paint peeled from the face of the building. Water seeped through growing cracks into the marquee, rotting it from the inside out. On the building's dark interior, aging plaster cracked and fell. Mice nibbled at the hemp staging ropes and took up residence between the springs inside the seats."

ABOVE: *After four decades as the Portsmouth Theatre and four more as the Civic, in June of 1985 the Music Hall returned to its original name. (GBP)*

On June 28, 1985, the old theater was sold again, this time to a group called the Portsmouth Civic Opera House, Inc. The buyers listed on the deed were Lewis Shaw, Gretchen and Jerry Weiss, and Sennon Nimetz. The team was known for restoring and adapting old Portsmouth buildings to modern uses. So far they had transformed two old schools into housing units, adapted a church into a restaurant, and repurposed the stately Kearsarge Hotel next door into a bar, a deli, and office space. Locals held their breath until the good news was revealed.

"Our original idea was to turn the thing into condominiums," Lewis Shaw later told *Sweet Potato*, a Maine-based arts publication. "But we just couldn't do it. We fell in love with this place."

"Our purpose is to produce popular entertainment at a profit," Jerry Weiss announced to the Portsmouth media following the sale. Bringing in big acts, the new owners explained, was the key to making their considerable investment in renovating the theater worthwhile. Blues guitarist B.B. King, singers Joan Baez

ABOVE: *Ongoing renovations in 1985 for the grand re-opening of the Music Hall as a performing arts center. The costly work was much greater than the new owners had anticipated. (GBP)*

OPPOSITE: *The removal of the 1901 dressing rooms, unused through most of the Civic years, evened out the size of the side wings. Adding a new dressing room block behind the stage allowed for an official Green Room, a larger room used by artists to gather and prepare before a performance. (GBP)*

and Tony Bennett, and jazz musician Dave Brubeck were being considered.

"We hope to expose our community to high caliber artists from other parts of the country," marketing director Sandi Mitchell said. Her words, echoing through the faded playhouse, sounded much like those of previous owner F.W. Hartford, who had boasted big city acts and first-run silent films. Mitchell made it clear that they were not going to ignore the wealth of local talent. "With this marvelous facility," she told the press, "we will encourage the development of our existing area arts groups."

One month after signing the purchase and sales agreement, Shaw and Mitchell sat with a reporter amid 900 empty orange chairs in the yawning dimly lit space. Down in the lobby a solo workman was peeling gunky strips of linoleum off the floor revealing a tiled surface not seen since World War II. A behemoth old Westinghouse air conditioner unit squatted in a corner ready to be trucked away and replaced.

ABOVE: *The decision to restore the Music Hall to its former glory was a daunting task for the new owners who planned to re-open the theater as a commercial venture bringing top acts to the Portsmouth stage once more. The cracked tiles of the newly uncovered lobby floor were among a host of renovation projects. (MHC)*

"Don't worry, we're going to paint the seats," Shaw told the reporter. "They won't be orange any more. The big job now is painting the ceiling."

Long curls of peeling paint quivered fifty feet overhead as four distant fans turned lazily. The original crystal chandelier that once hung in the center of the ceiling was gone, sold off or junked by people unknown. It had been replaced by a metal trash can lid studded with six light bulbs. Just renting the staging to reach the ceiling, it turned out, cost over $5,000.

The newspaper reporter scanned the whitewashed face staring three stories down from the center of the proscenium arch.

"That's Janus! He's the god of auspicious beginnings," the marketing director said, mistaking the Roman deity for his mythical buddy Bacchus. And unfortunately, as we will soon see, the two-headed Janus was also the god of sudden departures.

Respectful of the century-old building, the new owners were determined to preserve details like the original plaster friezes, the cast iron grill work, and the walnut balcony handrail. Lew Shaw and his team made extensive improvements including new exterior doors, a new ticket window, new lighting, and fire protection systems. They gutted and revamped the bathrooms, then cleaned up the second floor concession area. Backstage construction added seven new dressing rooms, showers, a production office, and a green room. The Civic sign came down and a new wooden marquee boldly proclaimed the return of the MUSIC HALL.

ABOVE: *Orange chairs salvaged from a fire at the Colonial Theatre (aka the Cinema) were installed at the Civic and repainted during the brief ownership of the Portsmouth Civic Opera House, Inc. (MHC)*

LEFT: *Festivals honoring Dionysus, the Greek god of all things festive, provided the perfect arena for staged storytelling to a large gathering. His image (or that of the Roman version, Bacchus) would later be a frequent design element in theaters all over the world. Formerly gold-leafed, but later painted white, the face at the peak of the Music Hall proscenium arch is affectionately known as "Frank" in honor of Frank Jones. (MHC)*

Open and shut

It was a black tie affair. The NH Symphony Orchestra performed "An Overture to the Seacoast" on opening night, October 26, 1985. Veteran Theatre by the Sea actor Scott Weintraub flew in from Los Angeles to host the ceremony. "The Music Hall will fill in the missing piece of the Portsmouth cultural puzzle," Weintraub told a packed audience. Mayor Eileen Foley declared "Portsmouth Music Hall Day" and the new owners gathered onstage for a rousing and lengthy standing ovation. The newspaper called the evening "a triumphant return of Portsmouth's last remaining performance hall."

BELOW: *The NH Symphony Orchestra performed at the gala opening night of the new, improved Music Hall on October 26, 1985. (MHC)*

After four decades as a declining old movie house, the Music Hall stage exploded with live action once more. With the Portsmouth Renaissance still half reality, half wishful thinking, the 1986-87 season shimmered with promise. Following opening night the kickoff musical acts included guitarist David Bromberg, the famed acapella group the Persuasions, a garage-rock band called The Del Fuegos, iconic trumpeter Dizzy Gillespie, and jazz fusion performers Spyro Gyra.

The new owners then booked a rising Chicago comedy troupe called The Second City, shifted to the Broadway musical *A Chorus Line*, tossed in top local performers, and added a classical music series along with the Boys Choir of Harlem. They rounded out the season with folk-pop music by Livingston Taylor, Christine Lavin, and New Hampshire's own Tom Rush.

"Talk around town says the Music Hall is in trouble . . . but the end is far from nigh," a *Portsmouth Herald* reporter wrote in February with the season still in progress. A critically acclaimed local production of *Peter Pan* had not covered its costs. A concert by rocker Steppenwolf sold out in a snowstorm on Thanksgiving, but an appearance by famed jazz trumpeter Dizzy Gillespie flopped. With construction costs already $200,000 over budget the owners were scrambling to find financing.

"It [theater] is not like building a shopping center, or a subdivision," partner Jerry Weiss told the *Herald*. "It's not perfect. We don't have all the bugs out."

"We're just trying different things to see what works and what doesn't," Lewis Shaw added. "It's too early to tell."

"We maybe were more audacious than we should have been," Weiss said prophetically. "But I think if we'd been more cautious, there wouldn't be a theater."

It was too much too soon for the hopeful investors. Ticket sales did not support the stellar performers, not to mention the price tag of advertising and promoting the opening season. Utility bills were staggering, adding to the seemingly endless restoration of crumbling brick walls and decaying floorboards. By the close of a single season the company balance sheet was $800,000 in the red. A public stock option soon failed.

In August 1986, little more than a year after they promised to save the Music Hall, the owners of Portsmouth Civic Opera

ABOVE: *The members of the Portsmouth Civic Opera Company strike a pose at their newly renovated Music Hall in 1985. (MHC)*

House, Inc. filed for bankruptcy. Their herculean effort left the building greatly improved. But it also left the impression that the obstacles to running a successful downtown theater were insurmountable. Falling back to their original plan, the owners told city officials that the only profitable future for the building was conversion to condominiums.

Sparked by the latest failure-to-launch and the condo threat, a grassroots team of volunteers dedicated to saving the old theater was gathering steam. Over 3,000 people signed a protest petition circulated by a group initially called "Don't Let the Hall Fall," led by Betsey Galligan, a soft-spoken mother of two and a former Civic usher. Members then asked locals to pledge five dollars to steward each historic brick. With approximately 40,000 bricks in each of the theater's four walls, there was enough potential revenue to expunge the lingering debt. Dollars trickled in.

Pressure mounted in September as a Massachusetts company, Stanhope Development Inc., expressed an interest in taking on the condo project, estimated at $3 million, plus $950,000 to purchase the building from its owners. Members of the city's Zoning Board of Adjustment balked at the developer's request for a variance to build twenty-nine condominium units in the old playhouse.

"This building is really no longer a theater," Stanhope's attorney said during a lengthy public hearing. "It's had its chance, and it just didn't work." Even the Portsmouth Chamber of Commerce agreed that creating residential units was a "reasonable" solution. Opponents including bar owner Jay Smith, Galligan, and attorney Gerald Zelin spoke powerfully against changing the zoning to allow development.

"My argument was pretty plain vanilla," Zelin says today. "I made the argument that just because the current owner wasn't able to turn a profit, didn't mean that no one could. I said it was premature to jump to the conclusion that this building was therefore worthless as a theater, which the zoning already permitted." When the Zoning Board of Adjustment unanimously turned down Stanhope's request for a variance to move forward with its condo plan, the owners sued the city.

By September, as the date of the bank foreclosure loomed, the optimistic group renamed "Friends of the Music Hall"

ABOVE: *Part of a sketch left on the wall of the Green Room by Disney animator Toby Bluth, director of the 1985 production of* Peter Pan. *Producers Roy and Eileen Rogosin brought in stars Nehemiah Persoff and Penny Peyser, among others, to join the cast of local actors. The critically acclaimed show, however, did not meet box office goals. (MHC)*

incorporated as a New Hampshire nonprofit agency. If they could raise $200,000, director Galligan announced, the group could demonstrate to investors that the performance space, if properly run, could still become a viable business and an economic boon to the city. The group hastily drafted a feasibility study to back up their claim. Emotions ran high. There was a clamor of public support, a series of well attended fundraisers, and two public forums marked by impassioned speeches.

"Where were all these people when we needed them?" a disappointed Lew Shaw told *NH Seacoast Sunday*. Plagued by lawsuits and debt collectors, the tall bearded developer worried that he and his partners were facing financial disaster. Shaw had even been arrested and taken from his home in handcuffs in front of his son for nonpayment of a $260 invoice, he told a reporter. "We made a Frankenstein for ourselves," owner Gretchen Weiss added. "It took over, and it's been a nightmare."

In a last ditch effort the Friends begged the Portsmouth City Council to buy the Music Hall and sell it to the nonprofit agency over five years. By a vote of five-to-three the council declined to spend tax dollars to save the iconic opera house. Then the clock ran out. Prime Meridian Bank foreclosed on the theater. Thankfully, the real estate market was experiencing a downturn that year. Legend says the bank decided not to raze the Music Hall because wrecking it would cost more than the property was worth.

Condo fever

So it was back to the auction block. On Wednesday, December 17, 1986, a Nashua, NH entrepreneur named Richard Cabral bought the Music Hall in what he called "a purchase of heart." Like owners F.W. Hartford, Frank Jones, and Elias Loew before him, Cabral was a wealthy, self-made businessman. By middle age Cabral had worked himself up from owning a single rental property to become the landlord of 700 inner-city apartments in fifty-eight Nashua buildings. By the time he purchased the Music Hall, Cabral's real estate empire had swelled to over 2,500

ABOVE: *Attendance fluctuated wildly during the experimental reboot of the Music Hall in 1985-86. While ticket sales for jazz icon Dizzy Gillespie (bottom) were disappointing, a concert by the Canadian-American rock band Steppenwolf (top) packed the house. Critics questioned whether Portsmouth was the right location for a commercial theater. Gillespie photo by Richard Godefroy. (WIK/MIS)*

rental units and he was branching out into land, office, and retail development.

With the collapse of Theatre by the Sea and the sale of the Music Hall to yet another real estate developer, in the summer of 1987 many wondered whether professional theater in Portsmouth was dead. Nancy Beck, a stalwart supporter of local arts and a TBS trustee, voiced her concerns bluntly to a reporter from the *Boston Sunday Globe*. "Is there a viable spot for theater in Portsmouth?" Beck asked. "Is Portsmouth a good place for theater in general?"

Even though the city's two big stages were silent, trained and talented performers were surviving, though not thriving, all around town. Generic Theater, Pontine Movement Theatre, Kitchensink Productions, and later Players' Ring were among the active Portsmouth troupes. The revamped Prescott Park Arts Festival continued to pack the summer months with plays and live music. And there was the new Portsmouth Academy of Performing Arts (PAPA), then located in the sprawling renovated Button Factory at the city's West End. PAPA was the creation of two "Hollywood refugees." Roy Rogosin was an experienced director, composer and playwright. His wife Eileen, a former Walt Disney television "Mouseketeer," was a talent agent, dancer, and acting teacher.

"I think it's a shame there has not been a successful community movement to save Portsmouth's two viable theaters," Roy Rogosin told the *Boston Globe*. "I think the city should have bought the Music Hall to save it from turning into condominiums. Eventually, some entrepreneur will buy a cow pasture in Greenland and put up an arena to service the area," he said.

The Music Hall had been closed for more than a year when Richard Cabral tried an experiment. The developer offered Ballet New England free use of the theater for eight holiday performances of *The Nutcracker* in December 1987. "Mr. Cabral wants to see how this goes," dance troupe manager Pat Carrico told the *Globe*. "He's interested in seeing whether there is support for the Music Hall and the performing arts on the seacoast. We're hoping there is."

"That theater was built for opera," Carrico said. "It's acoustically perfect. It's the last original theater in Portsmouth. If we lose it, we lose it forever."

The threat had never been more real. In a final effort to avoid bankruptcy, the previous owners had applied for a variance from the city to gut the old theater and install twenty-nine (later reduced to twenty-one) condominium units. There was precedent galore. All three twentieth-century downtown theaters — Arcadia, Olympia, and Colonial — had by this time been turned into office rental units. The Colonial, later the Cinema in the heart of Market Square, would eventually be torn down and replaced by an historic plaque. The Portsmouth Board of Adjustment, however, had refused to grant the condo variance. Portsmouth Civic Opera House Inc. then fought back and filed a lawsuit against the city.

When Cabral took over the Music Hall, he also took over the lawsuit to reverse the condominium ban. The legal battle for permission to turn the theater into luxury apartments was still pending in Rockingham Superior Court even as the ballet dancers performed *The Nutcracker* on the Music Hall stage that Christmas season. When reporters asked what would happen to the historic building in the coming year, the developer's attorney repeated — Mr. Cabral was keeping his options open. ❧

ABOVE: *Performances of* The Nutcracker *by Ballet New England became a popular holiday event at the Music Hall. This young dancer is preparing to appear in a production of* Swan Lake. *(ATH)*

CHAPTER 8

You've Got a Friend

The seacoast community steps up

"Your theater is haunting me," New York impresario Maude Hartwig wrote to Music Hall owner Justin Hartford after she toured the abandoned playhouse in 1942. But Hartwig's attempt to save the theater quickly turned to desperation. And yet, when Mary Kelley moved from the upper West Side of Manhattan to the seacoast in 1987, the Music Hall still cast the same powerful spell.

"Empty broken-down theaters are magic places, full of possibility and promise," Kelley says today. Already a veteran of thirty plays off and on Broadway, Kelley recalls that her first sight of Portsmouth's only surviving historic stage "moved me deeply." With her partner and future husband Tom Field, a theater lighting expert, Kelley joined the nascent Friends of the Music Hall, a small but resourceful group with a last-ditch plan to save the theater. Key members included commercial realtor and former Chamber of Commerce director David Choate III, future state representative and senator Martha Fuller Clark, photojournalist and pub owner Jay Smith, and Jameson French, a history major, conservationist, and businessman whose family had been in the lumber industry since the 1880s.

Looking back, the failure of the star-studded 1985-86 season under Lewis Shaw's team and their resulting bankruptcy was a wake-up call for seacoast residents. "Without that effort," dancer Drika Overton told *Seacoast Sunday*, "nobody would have realized

ABOVE: *Among the many artifacts uncovered during the theater restoration by the Friends of the Music Hall was this "miraculous medal" also known as a medal of Our Lady of Graces. It depicts the Virgin Mary, rays flying out from her hands, standing on a globe and crushing a serpent beneath her feet. (MHC)*

OPPOSITE: *Journalist and pub owner Jay Smith is remembered for his rich baritone singing voice and for his generous support of the Music Hall during its critical first years as a nonprofit institution. Photograph at the Press Room by Peter E. Randall (TPR)*

such a place existed. People felt the place hadn't been given a good shot." Like many culture lovers living in the seacoast, Overton channeled her disappointment into action by becoming a Friends of the Music Hall trustee.

Their Hail Mary strategy was simple. If the Music Hall could not survive as a profitable business, its final hope was to be a tax-exempt organization. The Friends had been approved as a 501(c)3 nonprofit by the Internal Revenue Service. Now all they needed was a ton of money to save the building before owner Richard Cabral turned it into luxury condominiums — or worse.

In April 1988 Cabral announced that he was losing money on the Music Hall and needed help. "It's probably the worst financial deal I've ever gotten into in my life," he told *Foster's Daily Democrat*. Insurance, maintenance, debt service, and taxes were costing him about two thousand dollars a week for a largely unused theater, the real estate mogul explained.

To keep the performing arts center open, Cabral said, he needed the city, a nonprofit group, or business partners to "step forward and share the burden." His attorney, Sanford Roberts, reminded newspaper readers that the previous developer's lawsuit to convert the theater into condos was still pending in Rockingham Superior Court. "While we're not going to dismiss it," Roberts warned, "neither are we going to move forward on it at this time." But the time bomb was ticking. In a few weeks, Cabral implied, he had to decide what to do with his theater.

On the same day that Cabral issued his call to action, a group of concerned citizens met to decide the fate of the ailing Theatre by the Sea. Should they turn the Bow Street facility into a community arts center? Should they sublet the space to an outside theater group? Or should they sell off their building, join forces with the Friends, and move into the old Music Hall?

"There was a feeling back then," Jameson French says, "that only one of the two theaters could survive." Supporters began to take sides. French, Martha Clark, David Choate, and Mary Kelley, who attended the pivotal Theatre by the Sea meeting, were drawn to save the historic 1878 playhouse.

The decision did not come easily. Martha Clark and her husband Geoff had been key supporters of the cutting edge performances at TBS from its inception. "We saw the play *Equus* in Boston. We saw *Equus* in New York City. The *Equus* at TBS was better than either one of them," she says.

Theatre by the Sea had put Portsmouth on the map and proven there was a hunger for the arts, the Clarks knew. But facts were facts. There was simply not enough space in the Music Hall for a resident acting company. And if that acting company failed, as had happened frequently during experiments in the 1940s, what would then become of the building? It was ultimately all about the building, Martha Clark says today, and what the building meant to the community. The Friends' plan called for putting the theater in a trust, separating the structure from the operating group, thus ensuring its survival.

"I went there to the Saturday afternoon movies all throughout my childhood when it was twenty-five cents for two tickets," Clark says. "And we would sit in the balcony and throw popcorn down on everyone."

"It's not just about saving iconic architecture," says Clark, a trained preservationist. "It's also about saving the history of all the interactions that went on in that space — Who got engaged sitting up in the balcony, who met their wife or husband there. So by saving the building, you also allow those memories to live

ABOVE: *Longtime Theatre by the Sea and Music Hall supporter Senator Martha Fuller Clark grew up sitting in the balcony watching movies at the Civic. Preserving the theater, she says, meant saving countless memories. (MHC)*

LEFT: *Buttons promoting Theatre by the Sea first located on Ceres Street, later on Bow Street, now Seacoast Rep. (ATH)*

on. I think that's what drove us, despite the risks, to take on the Music Hall project."

In response to Cabral's challenge, the Friends of the Music Hall quickly developed into a dynamic task force. Over the summer they drafted a "Plan for Success" designed to convince Cabral that the seacoast community was finally ready to support the struggling theater. Their detailed report included an operating budget, a mission statement, bylaws, a committee structure, and plans for an aggressive fundraising campaign.

"We were an interesting combination of community leaders and artistic people, particularly people who had been very involved with TBS," says business owner Chris Dwyer, who served as president of the Friends.

The Friends, however, had no intention of partnering with a real estate developer from Nashua. They intended to own the Music Hall outright. The proposed nonprofit theater group would be governed by a twenty-one-member Board of Trustees (later reduced to fifteen). Initially the plan included a tenuous merger with the ailing Theatre by the Sea, but that idea faded as TBS preserved its own stage on Bow Street that has since evolved into Seacoast Rep. These potent 1988 task force meetings also catalyzed the Seacoast Arts and Cultural Alliance (SACA) that grew to include over 300 artists and arts organizations.

Richard Cabral, at first, was cool to the idea of selling to the Friends — an idealistic all-volunteer nonprofit group — and he continued looking for more secure and lucrative backers to support his investment. In late July *NH Business Review* noted that the developer's "rocky romance with the city of Portsmouth has more sour notes than planners have regulations." Cabral's efforts to personally raise financial support for his Music Hall from local businesses, according to the financial news, had "bombed big time." Days later on August 3, Attorney Sanford Roberts sent David Choate a letter. His client was ready to sell.

ABOVE: *A popular parody poster by Ideaworks from the mid-1980s with this image read "Beautiful Downtown Portsmouth — Always a parking space." Photo collage by Ralph Morang. (JDR)*

OPPOSITE: *In a series of illustrations featuring famous movie monsters attacking Portsmouth, artist Bill Paarlberg captured the mood of an historic seaport in the 1980s where residents were both threatened and intrigued by the influx of tourists during the city's cultural and economic revival. In "Kongress Street" a giant ape climbs the North Church steeple in Market Square clutching a jet plane, a reference to the FB-111A that had recently crashed into a Portsmouth neighborhood. The Cinema movie theater is just below the monster's foot. Used by permission of the artist. (PAA)*

A grassroots victory

Success! On September 19, 1988, after tricky negotiations, the Friends proudly announced they had reached an agreement to buy the Music Hall from Richard Cabral. There would be no wrecking ball, unless the little volunteer group failed to pay the piper. They needed to secure a loan for $650,000 to reimburse Cabral's investment and repay the creditors of the previous owners. Bank Meridian agreed to the risky loan with one caveat.

To demonstrate that the public was truly ready to support the Music Hall, the Friends had to deliver a down payment of $200,000 within three months. Spearheaded by Jameson French, the accumulated private, public, and corporate donations poured in. But by the December 15 deadline, they were still $44,000 short. Thanks to an extension, on December 23, 1988, delegates

ABOVE: *This illustration of the Music Hall from the mid-1980s by Bill Paarlberg was often given as a gift to Friends of the Music Hall supporters. The surviving sign, as shown on the opposite page, is in the collection of the Music Hall. (PAA)*

from Friends of the Music Hall met with Bank Meridian with $194,000 in hand. Although they were still six thousand dollars shy, in a burst of holiday spirit, bank officials accepted their offer. Once again, the Music Hall passed into new hands.

Cautious optimism reigned. Having squeaked past a formidable bank deadline, the Friends faced an estimated $3.5 million fundraiser in the coming years. That's what it would take to restore the building, pay off the new mortgage, retire the old debt, and launch a fresh season of performances. "Three and a half million is nothing for Jamey," David Choate joked with his friend at a press conference. But everyone knew the task ahead was daunting.

On January 7, 1989, two weeks after acquiring the Music Hall, members of the task force gathered for a daylong retreat. "This is the beginning, not the end," an expert in nonprofit theaters told the group. In reality, the Friends had not yet saved the Music Hall. Their short term option with the bank had only taken the building "out of risk" for one year. There was still room to fail.

Now came the hard part. To truly save their beloved theater, the consultant explained, the Friends needed to sharply define their goals. It was time to build a powerful and insightful board of trustees, to find superior staff and volunteers, and to identify their future audience. They must book shows people wanted to see at a ticket price audiences were willing to pay. All this while restoring the aging structure and rapidly raising tons of money. There was no room for error this time around. Previous owners had complained that the 900-seat theater was too small for large acts and too large for small acts. The upcoming season, therefore, had to hit the precise mix of highly appealing shows at the lowest possible ticket cost. The mantra for the "new guard" became balance, stability, and don't-screw-up.

ABOVE: *The original sign from the early days of the Friends of the Music Hall era. (MHC)*

Fortune smiles

It was at this critical point in the modern history of the Music Hall that Bacchus, the Roman god of the theater who peers down from the proscenium arch, finally woke up. The survival of the building today owes much to the events that followed in 1989, even before the curtain rose on the initial Friends of the Music Hall season. The scrappy, untested, grassroots group had one advantage over every owner since the Peirce family in 1878. As a nonprofit organization, they could accept major tax-deductible gifts and grants. The big question was — who would donate? Hundreds of supporters had already chipped in to cover the down payment on the mortgage. How much money could a small community give?

First up, surprisingly, was Richard Cabral. The former owner's $75,000 gift, though generous, would arrive as installments over the next ten years. The bombshell announcement

BELOW: *The first large business donation of $100,000 from the Henley Corporation under Michael Dingman (center) was a game changer for the fledgling nonprofit group. Matching the "Henley Challenge" with many smaller donations inspired future private and corporate gifts that totaled millions of dollars. Friends of the Music Hall leaders David Choate III (left) and Jameson French were key drivers of the theater's early financial success. (GBP)*

came from the Henley Group of Hampton, an amalgam of thirty-five companies headed by financier and philanthropist Michael Dingman. Dingman had recently made headlines for taking his new company public at a record-breaking Wall Street offering of $1.2 billion, earning him the media nickname "deal-maker extraordinaire." On January 20, encouraged by Choate and French, Michael Dingman presented the Friends of the Music Hall with a giant check for $100,000.

"We look upon the restoration of the Music Hall as a regional activity," Dingman announced. "A flourishing Music Hall will enhance the performing arts and preserve a landmark." It was exactly the message the new owners wanted to send. Despite a flagging economy, the chairman of one of the most successful corporations in the seacoast was "investing" in the performing arts. Half the Henley money immediately went to pay down the principal on the theater mortgage, and the rest was earmarked for the upcoming performance season.

There was more. After the formal check-passing ceremony, in a surprise burst of excitement, Dingman pledged to match an additional $100,000 in small donations from the public. The "Henley Challenge" made headlines throughout the spring and summer as contributions mounted. The drama attracted more corporate underwriters and spurred the sale of "subscriptions" by which audience members could prepay for key seats to the much anticipated 1989-90 season.

"We would not have been able to make it without the Henley Challenge," says Martha Fuller Clark. "It gave us terrific leverage. We called around, people got excited and we were able to raise the money."

Within days of the Henley Challenge, as further proof the nonprofit strategy was building steam, ten architectural and engineering firms made an unprecedented offer. Working together, members of the newly-formed Portsmouth Architectural Collaborative agreed to create a comprehensive plan for renovating and restoring the theater. The report, valued at $50,000 of in-kind services, gave the Friends a blueprint for work that would take years to complete, but it also telegraphed a clear message.

"This is a community resource that demands community input," announced Jim Somes, a spokesman for the group. The plan, Soames told the press, also called for exterior improvements, a beautiful surrounding streetscape, and pedestrian walkways to be completed far in the future. By the twenty-first century, he correctly predicted, the reborn Chestnut Street venue would project a "theater district" atmosphere.

Last best chance

With executive director Mary Kelley and Tom Field at the helm and three full-time staffers on duty, a volunteer army worked nonstop through the spring and summer of 1989. Painters, electricians, plumbers, and cleaners labored, often for free. Skilled masons clambered up a tower of scaffolding to save the enormous endangered brick wall on Porter Street. New gutters healed the leaky pigeon-infested roof. A new marquee appeared. And for the first time the lobby, traditionally frigid in winter, received a supplementary heating system. Every nickel spent, Friends'

BELOW: *High above the city a worker tackles the restoration of the roof and gutters of the 1878 theater now owned by the nonprofit Friends of the Music Hall. (GBP)*

president David Choate made perfectly clear, came from funds on hand. There would be no hazardous borrowing against the mortgage this time around.

As the October 3 re-opening neared, often incompatible groups began to harmonize. The entire Seacoast was singing the same tune — our Music Hall must endure. Corporations, politicians, the media, the creative community, preservationists, banks, small companies, and the general public all knew the score. Having survived 111 years and dodged three condominium threats, Portsmouth's only historic theater was facing its last best hope of survival.

ABOVE: *New ropes and pulleys were replaced in the old fly system that works to this day much the way sailors of maritime Portsmouth hauled the sails of tall ships. (GBP)*

"This project will only work if we fill the seats," Choate said, and executive director Mary Kelley did the math. The opening season would include a weeklong run of two classic but costly stage plays, *My Fair Lady* and *Blithe Spirit.* To make a substantial return, the theater needed to sell 7,000 tickets. Audiences would also need to fill the house for Dave Brubeck, the Flying Karamazov Brothers, and the Boston Camerata. The upcoming season featured the Alvin Ailey dancers, the Preservation Hall Jazz Band, a Motown tribute, the NH Symphony, the Vienna Boys' Choir, and a live appearance by cast members of the *Sesame Street* television show.

The stars, at last, were perfectly aligned. The October 3 premiere was a triumph. "I'm so glad they saved the hall," jazz legend Dave Brubeck exclaimed at a champagne toast following a sold-out show. "For me, oh God, this is one of the greatest places I could play," Brubeck testified. "And I've played all the great halls." Over the next few years more vintage stars including singers Pearl Bailey and Carol Channing and pianist Victor Borge would agree.

Thanks to a burst of contributions, the $100,000 Henley Challenge surged $10,000 past its goal. With 9,000 tickets sold over the holidays, the Friends were in the black as 1990 dawned. In January, to reassure the public, David Choate held a press conference.

"A lot of people are concerned about the Music Hall," Choate said candidly. "They feel we'll be here today, gone tomorrow, as in the past. But that's not going to be the case." It would take at least two successful seasons, he agreed, to rebuild the theater's good name.

The regional press, equally convinced that the tide had turned, began to soften its language. The "failed and bankrupt" Music Hall of three years ago, in the shorthand of history, was now remembered fondly as a bold but undercapitalized and poorly promoted experiment. Fear of culture-eating condos and references to the Music Hall's "tumultuous past" dissolved. Reporters increasingly adopted the new upbeat phrase — "Portsmouth's landmark theater."

In hindsight, pundits theorized, it was the incredible acoustics of the high-domed ceiling that made the hall worth saving.

ABOVE: *Jazz master Dave Brubeck (1920–2012) praised the acoustics of the newly re-opened Music Hall as "one of the greatest places I could play." In 1954 Brubeck had been featured on the cover of* Time *magazine.*
(MIS)

It was, after all, one of the longest surviving theaters in the nation, not to mention one of the best performance stages in New England. Or was the revival due largely to the creeping gentrification of wealthy city dwellers? Or the city's unique location — equidistant from population centers like Boston, Portland, Manchester, and Concord? Perhaps the Music Hall was part of a larger nonprofit movement to restore old theaters like the 800-seat Monument-National (1893) in Quebec, the Grand Opera House (1884) in Macon, Georgia, and Colorado's Central City Opera House (1878).

Preservation architect Steve Roy, a Portsmouth native, saw a more seismic shift at play. It was a burst of youthful energy, Roy theorized, that saved the Music Hall. Drawn in by the city's cultural revival, Baby Boomers had settled in and around Portsmouth, developing careers, buying houses, having children, and establishing roots. For them, the Music Hall represented both the past and the future of the performing arts in their adopted hometown.

ABOVE: *In April 1989, in celebration of the year's astounding success and luck, the NH Symphony Orchestra performed once again. David Choate and Jameson French donned tuxedoes to introduce the show and to thank the community for its generosity, passion, and support. (GBP)*

ABOVE: *Built during the Frank Jones era, the back wall of the stage originally rested against another building. Constructed from "interior bricks" the massive wall had begun to deteriorate after the other building was removed leading to a huge and costly masonry repair project. (GBP)*

"Everybody claimed a few years ago that the Arts were dying," Roy said as the Friends of the Music Hall assumed the mantle of ownership. "But what's actually happened is that the people who were on the boards of directors then were people of my parents' generation. Look at the people on the boards now. They are now of my generation. I think what we experienced was a transition. I don't know whether the older people wouldn't let go or the younger generation wouldn't jump in, but that transition has now occurred."

It was Steve Roy, having restored historic structures all along the seacoast, who examined every nook and cranny of the Music Hall. His exhaustive list of repairs, published in the "Portsmouth Architectural Collaborative Report," put a price tag on preservation. Fixing the building would cost $1,391,500, not including work to the damaged slate roof. There was much to do.

When banks go bust

A funny thing happened on the way to the bank. On October 10, 1991, the Federal Deposit Insurance Company (FDIC) shut down seven New Hampshire banks, due largely to bad real estate loans. Bank Meridian of Hampton that held the Music Hall mortgage was among them. To avoid public panic, most of the banks were sold off in a group and re-opened the next day under a new name. The closures cost American taxpayers $996 million. For Music Hall president David Choate, however, it was manna from heaven.

"Our meeting with the FDIC was a huge, important, wonderful story in the history of the hall," Jameson French says today. "David and I were a sort of Mutt and Jeff combo, still are. I was able to raise funds, I guess, and he was the governance and badass business person."

In a nutshell, the Friends found themselves in a position to buy their mortgage back from the "bad bank" at a fraction of its cost. But first they had to find the cash. French had come to know Jay Smith, the handsome owner of the Press Room with the warm baritone singing voice. They talked, and despite his beat-up red Toyota and thrifty lifestyle, Smith confided that he had the financial means to help out.

"I will give you a line of credit on my trust fund for up to $250,000 if you can negotiate with the FDIC," Jay Smith told French. "I don't have a family, Jamey. I can do this, just don't let anybody except David know."

French recalls the day, with Smith's promised loan in hand, that they drove to Bedford to play poker with the feds.

"I was a wreck," he says. "I was thinking, God, we're going to throw this thing away, we're going to lose it." Choate brought

ABOVE: *Ironically the city's oldest theater, the Music Hall, has survived while the competing Franklin, Arcadia, Olympia, and Colonial theaters are gone. This candid shot shows the brick walls of the Cinema (formerly the Colonial) being eaten away by a demolition crew at the end of the twentieth century. (MIS)*

the keys to the Music Hall and placed them on the table. Did the FDIC really want to close down a beloved historic theater and turn it into a parking garage? Choate never blinked. The bank caved.

The Friends were able to pay off their mortgage that day at a savings of roughly $350,000. Following a vigorous fundraiser, they quickly repaid the "anonymous" Jay Smith and the nonprofit theater was debt free.

"I don't think the Music Hall would ever have made it if that hadn't happened," French says today. Jay Smith later gifted much of the money back to the theater. The identity of the anonymous lender remained a secret until Jay Smith's untimely death in 2002, when it was revealed at a standing-room-only gathering in his memory at the Music Hall.

Butting heads

It was one thing to pull off a miracle, quite another to sustain it. By the mid-1990s, according to a Music Hall executive memo, "the blush is off the rose." Staff members were increasingly at odds with board members over programming. Reliable volunteers were getting harder to find. Fundraising and ticket sales were slightly off target. Pleasing all of the people all of the time had gotten even harder since the *Boston Globe* declared the restored theater had become "the beating cultural heart of the New Hampshire seacoast."

"Frankly a lot of the time when I was president of the board I was mediating," Chris Dwyer recalls. People focused on delivering great performances were frequently at odds with the "bottomline people," Dwyer says, who were focused on finances and real estate.

"Can we afford to do this? What will happen if we do that? It was all very exciting," she says. "Remember, these were pretty high-powered people to be on a board of a small arts organization. And I felt it was my role to keep them talking and balancing these ideas."

"I literally was sometimes standing between two guys screaming at each other," Dwyer adds. "And I think that's

ABOVE: *Press Room owner Jay Smith insisted on keeping his financial support of the nonprofit Music Hall a secret. His contribution was only revealed following his untimely death at age 65 in 2002 during a standing-room-only memorial service at the theater. Photo by Joe Stevens. (JSP)*

probably a stage in the development of an organization like the Music Hall. You had to keep butting heads on those things because you had to keep a vision alive, but you couldn't go only on vision."

The stirring salvation of the Music Hall had given way to a laundry list of critical, but not-very-sexy, tasks. A new sprinkler system, for example, put the building fully in compliance with modern safety codes for the first time. A new elevator made performances handicapped accessible. The brick exterior on Chestnut Street, now newly painted in an "historically plausible" pinkish-cream color, was festooned with four colorful, hanging banners. Each banner boldly proclaimed the theater's mission to deliver the very best in DANCE, MUSIC, FILM, and THEATRE.

ABOVE: *The nonprofit owners proudly proclaimed the mission of the new, improved Music Hall on the exterior wall repainted in an "historically plausible" pinkish-cream color. Millions of dollars worth of work still lay ahead to stabilize and renovate the building. (MHC)*

Maintenance teams made extensive backstage repairs. They modernized lighting and sound equipment, replaced balcony seats, and enhanced the exterior brick streetscape — all subtle evidence that the nonprofit experiment was working. Volunteer board members logged countless meeting hours and churned out reams of memos, reports, balance sheets, and strategic plans. To recoup a $750,000 annual programming budget, Music Hall officials knew, was a dizzying prospect. To balance the books they needed to stage more local acts and children's shows, triple the number of prepaid subscribers, find fresh corporate sponsors, reel in maximum grant money, and increase theater rentals.

Like jugglers in a vaudeville act, the Friends had to keep the show going even as the world transformed around them. A dozen Portsmouth dance clubs were giving way to brewpubs and designer coffee shops. Fashion turned casual, music went grunge, and the newborn internet was changing everything. Cell phones and pagers vibrated, DVDs replaced videotapes, and the rising tide of a new thing called "email" poured in. The Portsmouth Chamber of Commerce branded the proliferation of new high-tech companies as "The eCoast."

The Shipyard Project

The closure of Pease Air Force Base in 1991, meanwhile, signaled a seismic seacoast shift from a military economy to an even greater reliance on tourism, small business, and the service industry. After a weak start, the defunct 4,365 acre air base, renamed Pease Tradeport, would become a thriving industrial center with over 14,000 employees. Portsmouth's population, however, would drop almost 5,000 residents to roughly 21,000.

With the exception of Woodrow Wilson, Franklin D. Roosevelt, and John F. Kennedy, New Hampshire had voted exclusively for Republican presidents since 1856. Then in the 1990s the Granite State suddenly turned blue. Portsmouth was earning a reputation as a Democratic stronghold. So back in the '90s, news that the Portsmouth Naval Shipyard was once again on the federal base-closure list heightened fears that blue-collar conservative Portsmouth was on life support. The city's population was

growing wealthier, increasingly educated, and more liberal. Not everyone was pleased with the trend. And not everyone liked opera, jazz, ballet, classical music, or symphonies. Once home to minstrelsy, vaudeville, and discount movies, the Music Hall, detractors moaned, was becoming an elitist institution for rich snobs.

That attitude was greatly ameliorated by nine barefoot dancers, aged twenty-four to seventy-one, who first took to the Music Hall stage in the fall of 1994. The renowned Liz Lerman Dance Exchange had come from Washington, DC, to Portsmouth at the theater's invitation. Their goal was to translate the 200-year history of Portsmouth Naval Shipyard into art. For two years the seemingly impossible task, funded by a $145,000 grant, galvanized the community. What many locals saw as "a

ABOVE: *Founded in 1800 in the Age of Sail, even after two centuries the Portsmouth Naval Shipyard on the Maine side of the Piscataqua River was seen by many as an inaccessible and secretive place where warships were once built and submarines are now repaired. (JDR)*

ABOVE: *After years of research as part of the Shipyard Project members of the Liz Lerman Dance Exchange translated the movements of navy yard workers and legends of the region's maritime history into movement in a series of performances that involved and inspired the entire community. (GBP)*

remote, cold, industrial place" for building warships and repairing nuclear submarines, blossomed into a hothouse of stories and movement.

"We're trying to embrace an element of the community that does not necessarily associate themselves with the Arts," a spokesperson for the Music Hall said. "It will also raise awareness during a time when the whole destiny of the shipyard is in question."

Choreographer Liz Lerman and her troupe met with dozens of shipyard workers and officials. They connected with hundreds of volunteers and listened to countless stories of the city's seafaring history. Mayor Eileen Foley, who had served as a painter's assistant at the shipyard during World War II, told her story. Gerald McLees, a survivor of the sunken USS *Squalus* submarine also shared personal tales. Shipyard Commander Peter Bowman was so intrigued by the power of the Arts to build community that he joined the Music Hall board of directors.

Dancers in the Shipyard Project incorporated movements and gestures made by skilled workers, and integrated the motion of ships and machinery with oral histories. What began with considerable eye-rolling, skepticism, and apathy, Lerman later admitted, is remembered today as a powerful and emotional synthesis of history, community, artistry, and industry.

"The shipyard is a place of immense creativity, collaboration, and performance — much like a small modern dance company," Liz Lerman wrote years later in her memoir. The final Dance Exchange performances, staged at the Music Hall and across the seacoast, "captured the soul of the shipyard," one critic wrote. Strange as it might seem, a diverse community had made contact with its shared maritime past through stories and through dance.

The take-home message was far-reaching. If the Arts could heal, educate, and sustain an entire community, then artists might be as essential to that community as bankers and business owners, teachers and truck drivers, police and politicians. And if artists were then essential to a thriving society, who sustains the theaters, large and small, where these artists perform? Having saved their landmark theater, the Friends of the Music Hall now faced the toughest challenge of all — staying alive.

A new millennium

Through thick and thin, as Portsmouth careened into a new millennium the Music Hall continued to deliver great acts. From classic names like Carol Channing, The Coasters, Chet Atkins, and Patti Page, to Joan Baez and Judy Collins — the music rang out. Seacoast audiences toured the world with George Winston, Bruce Hornsby, the Irish Rovers, Buckwheat Zydeco, Suzanne Vega, Ladysmith Black Mambazo, John Hiatt, Wynton Marsalis, Philip Glass, and Natalie MacMaster. There was no end of opera, Shakespeare, comedy, kids' shows, classical music, and ballet — so many celebrities interspersed with local talent.

Jeffrey Gabel, the executive director during this period, was a Pennsylvania native with a unique background. He arrived

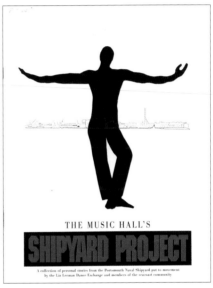

ABOVE: *(top) "Seems to me," renowned choreographer and teacher Liz Lerman told crowds gathered at the Portsmouth Naval Shipyard in the mid-1990s, "that art can play a much bigger role in people's lives than it does." Photo by Lise Metzger. (LIZ)*

ABOVE: *(bottom) A playbill for the concluding performance of the Shipyard Project at the Music Hall. (MHC)*

in Portsmouth after working in public television and playing Chuckles the Clown on *Mister Rogers' Neighborhood* television show. Gabel became the ideal ringmaster. Artistic director Jane Forde, meanwhile, was an award-winning choreographer and teacher who had danced in London, at the White House, and at the Kennedy Center.

"Jeff and Jane made the Music Hall beloved in the community," says Gail VanHoy Carolan, who currently directs fundraising for the theater. And it wasn't only the live performances that brought the community together.

"It was also the return of the movies every night that made us the beating heart of the city again," recalls Chris Dwyer, who presided over the board of directors at the time. "There were a lot of single people living downtown then. Women were saying it was okay to go to the Music Hall on their own at night rather than hit the bar scene."

ABOVE: *Throughout the 1990s and into the twenty-first century the Friends of the Music Hall mixed classic acts with the latest musicians and performers to create a solid reputation. The return to movie nights harkened to the days when the first silent films played along with traveling vaudeville acts. (MHC)*

Unlike the early twentieth century when there were as many as five downtown movie houses, now there was only one. And yet, despite all the nightly action, there was never enough income.

"Nonprofits do the Lord's work," Gabel once told a reporter. "They take on tasks that no one else wants to do because they are too hard, too unglamorous, or too unprofitable." The biggest challenge, he said, was "money, always money. Nonprofits don't make money, they bleed it."

"Yes, there were a lot of rescue missions during that time," Dwyer admits. "We had to do several back-to-Jesus missions with the board over money. I remember at one point we learned we had to raise a quarter of a million dollars right away, and we did. The truth is — the Music Hall wasn't saved once, it was saved many, many times." ❧

ABOVE: *The creation of the nonprofit Friends of the Music Hall saved the 1878 theater from destruction in the 1980s. History proves the Music Hall has been saved many times by countless people. Here many of the original "Friends" strike a pose in the Founders Lobby. Front row, left to right: Deborah Chag, Mary Kelley, Elizabeth Richards, Martha Fuller Clark, Christine M. Dwyer, Lee D. Vander-mark, Ann Kendall, Rebecca B Marden. Back row, left to right: Kathleen Watson, Norman R. Ritter, David E. Choate III, Jameson French, Thomas H Field, Dean Diggins, Barbara Gutin, Drika Overton, Michael Chubrich, Nancy Phillips. (MHC)*

CHAPTER 9

Begin Again

A fresh vision and a dazzling future

One hundred and twenty-five years after the Hon. William Hackett addressed the theater's first audience, his words rang out on the Music Hall stage again. "A community is known by the character and place of its amusements," a Hackett re-enactor in a swallowtail coat announced in 2003. "This place will exert a refining influence upon those who occupy it."

Hackett's prediction of January 29, 1878 was fully realized. A community had come together at a critical moment to keep the theater open and the performing arts alive. They had shared, in Hackett's words, "those recreations which enliven, sweeten, and lengthen life." And with each performance the members of that community had grown closer, more interested in, and more respectful of one another. They were becoming a family.

That reality was never more evident than in the fall of 2003 when the Friends of the Music Hall recreated the theater's opening night jubilee. Prior to the festivities, costumed guides offered a tour of the historic building, pointing out the original tile floor, leather-covered doors, decorative carvings flecked with gold leaf, and swatches of early wallpaper, frescoes, and stencil work. In a rare peek backstage, visitors gazed up five stories at the old hemp fly system installed by the same craftsmen who built the city's tall ships. The remnants of an elevator that once hoisted actors to their dressing rooms thirty feet above the stage were still visible.

ABOVE: *A Music Hall staff member in Victorian attire waves to audience members during the "125th Jubilee" celebrating the opening of the Music Hall in 1878. (MHC)*

OPPOSITE: *The twenty-first century brought new leadership, new vision, and a $13.5 million fundraising goal to revitalize and rebrand the Music Hall as the hub of world-class programming in the region. Here Ray LaMontagne performs with John Stirratt on the Portsmouth stage. (DJM)*

Despite a rainy evening, on October 4 the entrance to the Music Hall was transformed into a nineteenth-century street scene. Flower and candy pedlars hawked their wares. A young "newsie" sold souvenir copies of the Portsmouth daily paper. With onlookers distracted by a man juggling apples, a pickpocket made his move, but the boy was chased off by a mustachioed "copper" wielding his truncheon.

Inside the theater women in voluminous Victorian gowns and long white gloves sipped glasses of punch dipped from a crystal bowl. Men in top hats and tuxedos made way for wandering musicians in the densely packed lobby. Following Mr. Hackett's introduction, a troupe of professional actors directed by Genevieve Aichele reprised the slapstick farce *Mr. Wopps* and the three-act satire *Caste*. The first two plays ever seen on the Music Hall stage were back. With the lights dimmed and the audience in vintage attire, it was 1878 once more.

Challenge and change

Three days after the historic jubilee, workmen excavating for a sewer line hit a hexagonal coffin in the west lane of Chestnut Street a block from the Music Hall. Archaeologists uncovered the remains of thirteen ancient burials. DNA testing proved what historians had long suspected, that Portsmouth's only African Burying Ground had been forgotten, paved over, and built upon as the city expanded. Set aside in the 1700s by town decree, the segregated graveyard had been located only a few yards from Portsmouth's colonial almshouse and prison further up Chestnut Street, now the site of the Music Hall. Today a memorial park at the site of the lost cemetery is the highlight of Portsmouth's Black Heritage Trail. Around here, the past is never far away.

The 125th anniversary also stands out as the year the federal government acknowledged the importance of the theater. Following negotiations with state Senator Judd Gregg, the Music Hall was nominated to the "Save America's Treasures" campaign. The award came with a $395,000 matching grant from the National Park Service and the National Trust for Historic Preservation.

ABOVE: *A Victorian flower girl welcomes visitors at the 2003 recreation of the opening of the historic Music Hall by the Peirce family.* (MHC)

"It turns out that Judd Gregg and his wife Kathy had their first date watching *Gone With the Wind* at The Music Hall," says Douglas Nelson, a long-time Music Hall trustee. "This grant was the seed money for the eventual $13.5 million restoration of the old hall, plus the acquisition and renovation of The Loft in years to come." Those years to come, however, would fall under a new administration.

"This has been the best job I have ever had in my life," Music Hall executive director Jeffrey Gabel announced in 2003. But after five challenging years at the helm, he was moving to Pennsylvania to restore the nonprofit Majestic Theater at Gettysburg College.

The local media made much ado about the fact that the Music Hall, Strawbery Banke Museum, and Prescott Park Arts Festival were all losing their executive directors at the same moment. "The town is falling apart," a local museum employee told the *Boston Globe*. "Is It a Sign of the Times?" another newspaper asked.

"There is no conspiracy," said Jameson French, who had served as a trustee for all three organizations. The trio of departures, he

ABOVE: *Supporters gather at the site of the African Burying Ground in Portsmouth following a concert by the Soweto Gospel Choir at the Music Hall. Both historic locations are located on Chestnut Street. (DJM)*

ABOVE: *One of the first programs established by the Friends of the Music Hall, the School Days Series, introduces thousands of children to theater every year. (GBP)*

told reporters, was only an unfortunate coincidence. Portsmouth was growing up and the next generation of executive directors would face many challenges during tough economic times.

Every nonprofit board of directors, French pointed out in an interview, must steer that institution to fulfill its stated mission while meeting its financial goals. Finding the right director, therefore, was the board's most important task.

"These individuals tend to be idealistic and believe passionately in the cause they represent," French said. The new director had to be a keen decision maker, a CEO to the staff, and a perpetual fundraiser. He or she must also deal with an ever-changing volunteer board while being the public face of the entire organization. Locating each perfect director, French said, would require "an alignment of the stars."

Filtered through the local newspaper, the search for these key nonprofit directors was a nearly impossible "treasure hunt" to

fill three "thankless jobs." According to former Music Hall president Chris Dwyer, however, this seemingly precarious situation was a boon.

"What it did was give everybody a fresh start," Dwyer recalls. "Those moments can be really healthy, particularly in the Arts where people are scrambling for the same dollars. It was actually very helpful to be able to have all those changes at the same time."

The out-of-towner

In September of 2003, on the eve of their 125th anniversary jubilee, board members announced the formation of a search committee to find their next executive director. "The Music Hall has dodged more bullets than Clint Eastwood," arts and culture reporter Chris Elliott wrote, and it would certainly survive this latest crisis thanks to "good fortune and good citizens."

ABOVE: *Music Hall staff members welcome their new executive director with open arms in 2004. (MHC)*

On March 31, 2004, after a six-month review of over sixty candidates, search committee chair Peter Bowman, a former commander at the Portsmouth Naval Shipyard, broke the news. The new Music Hall executive director was a lively red-haired Midwesterner named Patricia Lynch. The founder of Brass Tacks Theatre, a venue for inventive alternative plays in Minneapolis, Lynch had also successfully run The O'Shaughnessy, a performing arts center at St. Catherine University's campus in St. Paul. As an award-winning playwright, a poet, and a director, as well as a fundraiser and theater manager, Lynch's resumé and her energy "wowed the staff and the search committee," Bowman said.

From the get-go, Lynch embraced the idea that Portsmouth's oldest theater could become its biggest cultural attraction and a key economic driver. "The Music Hall is uniquely placed to play a growing role in the seacoast community," she said at her introductory press conference. But first, the out-of-towner needed to spend a month exploring the region, getting to know its people, and engaging in "dynamic conversations" with her new colleagues at the theater, she said.

Despite its rocky history, the Music Hall had come a long way in the century since F.W. Hartford ran the theater with one part-time manager. The new director inherited a staff of twelve who had staged more than thirty major shows on an annual budget of $1.6 million. By 2004 an estimated 870 seacoast residents made their living in nonprofit arts groups, and that figure did not count freelance artists and performers. Those nonprofit employees added $26 million to the region's economy each year, a value that would double in the coming decade and continues to rise. Tourism among New Hampshire's lakes, mountains, and seacoast, plus high-tech or "smart manufacturing" were fast becoming the dominant industries in New Hampshire. The stage was set, according to a cover story in a local arts publication, for Lynch to "write the next act for the Music Hall" and lead the landmark theater into the future.

"Everything comes back to vision," Lynch told the *Wire* in her first major Portsmouth interview. Once people understand that vision, she explained, they will understand that investing in the arts is the same as investing in their community and in themselves.

ABOVE: *A playwright, a poet, and a director from the Midwest, Patricia Lynch was selected as the new executive director in 2004. (DJM)*

"If you care about your children, you'll expose them to the Arts," she said. "If you want a better economic center because you're a business person, you'll invest in the Arts." Achieving her grand vision, she admitted in the spring of 2004, would require fully engaged corporate donors, philanthropists, and committed business sponsors. Success would take a village.

Portsmouth has long been wary of outsiders, often dubbed "carpetbaggers," for fear they might exploit the city's resources and then disappear. In fact, however, it has often been outsiders who manned Portsmouth's tall ships, flew its fighter jets, piloted its nuclear submarines. Outsiders built our bridges, launched profitable companies, started restaurants, constructed hotels, and serviced the city's hospitality industry.

Outsider money and influence, in fact, had saved all of the historic house museums in Portsmouth from destruction in the twentieth century. And while the ancient Peirce family put up the initial cash to build the Music Hall, it was people who came from elsewhere — including Frank Jones, F.W. Hartford, and Elias Loew — who ultimately invested in, improved, and kept the theater open. That's not to mention the countless thousands of people from across the globe who have provided the entertainment and bought the tickets that kept the theater lively.

Baby steps

The *Portsmouth Herald* welcomed Patricia Lynch warmly, yet warily. "While we eagerly anticipate her vision," *Herald* editors wrote, "we ask that she keep one thing in mind: Portsmouth loves its Music Hall . . . It's our baby. We urge you to be careful with our baby, Ms. Lynch."

The baby metaphor works, but only briefly. As a full-on arts professional, the new executive director had every intention of raising the Music Hall to a more mature, more vibrant and advanced stage. And she knew that the changes would raise eyebrows.

"The people I met when I interviewed were incredibly interesting and smart," Lynch recalls fifteen years later. "What was missing in Portsmouth, for me, was an anchor arts organization.

I wanted world-class programming — I hate that overused phrase. Let's say I was aiming for programming that punches at a higher weight class than the Music Hall was used to."

"It seemed like Portsmouth was on its way to becoming one of those very special places in America where everyone wants to live and work and play," Lynch says today. "It had the architecture, great food, all that history, the cool people, and a natural beauty. It had an authentic character of its own, and I knew the Music Hall could make it even better."

The most successful program in place when the new director arrived was the annual "Telluride by the Sea." In 1999 Bill and Stella Pence, co-founders of the prestigious Telluride Film Festival, retired from the mountains of Colorado, to the flat seaside of Portsmouth. In collaboration with the Music Hall, they created a much smaller, but equally intimate and immersive, film event in New Hampshire. The three-day festival featured six as-yet-unreleased movies hand-picked directly from their Colorado premiere. Then, as now, movie buffs queued around the block, dined out in downtown Portsmouth, joined discussion groups, and attended opening-night and film wrap parties.

"It's a different experience to see a film for which there is little or no baggage," Bill Pence said one early Telluride night at

ABOVE: *Bill and Stella Pence, co-founders of the Telluride Film Festival in Colorado brought their idea to New England as "Telluride by the Sea," one of the most successful and enduring annual events at the Music Hall. They are seen here with Music Hall Film Coordinator Chris Curtis. (DJM)*

the Music Hall. "It's wonderful to look at them with virgin eyes and make your own decisions."

Thanks to "Telluride by the Sea," the former Civic was finally able to shed its twentieth-century reputation as a creaky, leaky, discount movie parlor with sticky floors and occasionally questionable fare. The annual post-Labor Day event at the new improved Music Hall, in contrast, was fresh, chic, global, and cutting edge. And the excitement continues every year.

Director Lynch also inherited a theater beloved by the community. Former director Jeff Gabel and artistic director Jane Forde, both seasoned performers, had managed to heal a long-standing riff between the hall and local artists. The ongoing success of the Music Hall, it has been suggested, also helped build a wider marketplace for local performers who established their own brand and set up smaller independent venues around the city.

The impact of Liz Lerman's Shipyard Project continued to resonate across the seacoast for years, inspiring a host of collaborative arts projects. One of them, an original play entitled

ABOVE: Entertained by a live band, film buffs line up on the red carpet for the gala opening of the three-day annual "Telluride by the Sea" festival. (DJM)

Neighborhoods, involved forty community members aged seven to seventy-seven. Drawn from deep research and oral histories, the play explored how historic events like the arrival of the railroad, immigration, and urban renewal had changed the lives of real people in Portsmouth. Genevieve Aichele of the NH Theatre Project wrote, produced, and directed the play that was staged for free at the Music Hall.

"For me, Portsmouth will always be the city I discovered when creating and performing *Neighborhoods*," Aichele says roughly twenty years later. "Through the project I learned that much of the undercurrent of unrest I felt while living here stemmed from the urban renewal of the 1960s that tore communities apart. The past affects the future. Through community theater, in our own small way, I think we were able to repair a bit of the damage."

The new director also inherited the "Save America's Treasures" federal grant that kick-started a decade-long capital campaign to restore the theater building. "When the Music Hall comes calling, dig deep," the *Portsmouth Herald* editors urged its readers. It was not only restaurateurs and retailers who benefited each time the 900-seat theater had a sold out show, the newspaper editorialized. "The Music Hall is a cultural rallying point — a fixture in our creative community." And since entrepreneurial business people are drawn to live among other creative people, the theater was essentially populating the seacoast with its own future benefactors.

No one remembers this period better than Gail VanHoy Carolan. Coming from a business career, Carolan had been on the Music Hall board barely three months when she found herself the chairperson. When Jeff Gabel suddenly resigned, for the next year she was effectively in charge of running a theater, fundraising, and finding a new director. "With a notoriously hard working board and a ready and able staff we flew the plane," she says looking back. "It was a fun and insane time."

"We were at a point where every time we would get a member, we would lose one. We were just spinning our wheels. We could never get traction," Carolan says. "That was a big transition point, recognizing that, okay, we're going to step it up here. We needed to transition from a board-led organization to a professional one."

"We knew we needed to have branded programming so that we wouldn't have the same customer all the time," she continues. "We needed to get really diversified and build membership, but the only marketable brand we had was 'Telluride by the Sea.' Then Patty came in with her binder of ideas and a plan for a writer's program, and we knew we had our candidate."

Writers on stage

Lynch's first innovation was a triumph. In November 2005, "Writers on a New England Stage" premiered with the celebrated TV, film, and Broadway star Alan Alda, best known for his role in the hit comedy series *M*A*S*H*. The format, unchanged to this day, called for the author — this was Alda's first book — to read a little, then settle into a comfy chair to be interviewed by a host from NH Public Radio, initially Laura Knoy

BELOW: *NH Public Radio host Virginia Prescott interviews novelist and Music Hall supporter Dan Brown during an episode of "Writers on a New England Stage." House band Dreadnaught provides the music. (DJM)*

NEVER HAVE YOUR DOG STUFFED
ALAN ALDA
'Honest, touching and very funny – like Mr Alda himself'
David Mamet, author of *Glengarry Glen Ross*

ABOVE: *From the very first reading by Alan Alda, "Writers on a New England Stage" established Portsmouth as a literary destination for top book authors. Best known for his role in the TV war-comedy-drama* M*A*S*H, *Alda read from his first book* Never Have Your Dog Stuffed. *(RAN)*

and later Virginia Prescott. The author then answered questions supplied by audience members, many of whom were clutching autographed copies of his book. Dreadnaught, the hard-charging house band, performed between segments. Days later, the entire event was broadcast and podcast on Public Radio.

"My mother didn't try to stab my father until I was six," Alan Alda began reading. The audience gasped, and a new chapter of the Music Hall was born. Alda's first memoir, *Never Have Your Dog Stuffed: And Other Things I've Learned*, went on to become a bestseller. Patricia Lynch recalls how, behind the curtain, she asked the celebrated actor for advice on how to relax before stepping on stage. "Dance!" Alan Alda told her, and they did.

Years later the director got to dance offstage with horror novelist Stephen King as the house band played "Don't Fear the Reaper." Lynch watched as U.S. Secretary of State Madeleine Albright played the drums with the band. The executive director sang songs with historian David McCullough. She got writing tips from novelists like Elmore Leonard, E.L. Doctorow, and Salman Rushdie. She waited nervously as Supreme Court Justice Sonya Sotomayor battled her way through an epic New England snowstorm to arrive in the nick of time.

Getting the writers project off the ground was scary. "We had no idea if it was going to work," Lynch says. "When I went to New York to pitch the series, I was asked repeatedly — where exactly is Portsmouth, New Hampshire?"

It's not name-dropping to tout the famous people who have since joined the "Writers on a New England Stage" guest list. It's just show business. The Music Hall has seen its share of literary celebrities from Mark Twain to Portsmouth's own Celia Thaxter and Thomas Bailey Aldrich. The success of "Writers" is deeply tied to the early Portsmouth Lyceum era that drew audiences of the nineteenth century. Hundreds gathered on the same site in the old "Temple" to tap into the wisdom of speakers including black abolitionist Frederick Douglass and transcendentalist Ralph Waldo Emerson.

The idea then, as now, was to bring the greatest minds, up close and personal, into the heart of the seacoast community. That guest list now includes book authors Judy Blume, Simon Winchester, Lee Child, Jodi Picoult, Joyce Carol Oates, Doris

Kearns Goodwin, Patti Smith, Erik Larson, Dave Barry, Tom Brokaw, Patricia Cornwell, John Irving, Joan Didion, Anna Quindlen, Ann Patchett, P.J. O'Rourke, Jeffrey Toobin, Neil Gaiman, Ken Burns, Cokie Roberts, Isabel Allende, Diana Gabaldon, Barbara Kingsolver, Malcolm Gladwell, John Updike, and many more. Publishers and literary agents no longer ask where Portsmouth is located.

"This is some remarkable town," author Mitch Albom commented after his appearance, "where 900 people come out on a Friday night for a book reading."

In 2005 Dan Brown, a lifetime seacoast New Hampshire resident, made a rare public appearance to talk about his controversial novel. *The Da Vinci Code* was even then being adapted into a Hollywood film, the first in a series starring Tom Hanks as "symbologist" Robert Langdon. Despite a firestorm of criticism and lawsuits, the book would sell eighty million copies

Executive Director Patricia Lynch interviews Deepak Chopra, Indian-born American author, public speaker, alternative medicine advocate, and prominent figure in the New Age movement. (DJM)

in forty-four languages. "If anyone wants to sue me, we have forms in the back," Brown joked. He returned to the Music Hall with each bestseller and has since become an important theater benefactor.

Another time Brown was in the audience, sitting in the front row with Stephen King and King's son, author Joe Hill. The trio had come to hear Margaret Atwood read from her latest bestseller. "If lightning strikes this theater tonight," someone quipped, "the American publishing industry is doomed."

ABOVE: *During a "Writers on a New England Stage" appearance by bestselling author Margaret Atwood, members of the Music Hall audience that evening included thriller novelist Dan Brown, horror writer Stephen King, and his son, author Joe Hill. (DJM)*

Revolutionary renovation

The vision was now blazingly clear — restore the landmark theater to its golden-era glory and pack the hall with 24-carat acts. Still basking in the glow of their new literary lecture series, in July of 2006 the Friends of the Music Hall unveiled the renovated proscenium arch and stage. The gold-leafed features had been "modernized" by post-World War II owner Guy Tott, whose workers had covered them in thick coats of white paint. In Phase One of an immense project, under the direction of TMS Architects, experts meticulously cleaned and revived the ornamentation. A forgotten mural, uncovered by workers, inspired one *Boston Globe* reporter to pen this rapturous review:

"Freshly painted golden leaves sparkle around the stage that in the past showcased Buffalo Bill Cody, Mark Twain, and John Philip Sousa. Chubby-cheeked cherubs cavort across a turquoise sky above a gilded visage of Dionysus. The gods are smiling down on the Portsmouth Music Hall," the *Globe* announced. The restoration also inspired the Indigo Girls, an America folk rock duo, to pen a moving ballad, "Mariner Moonlighting," about the theater's haunting beauty.

In Phase Two workers tackled the capacious auditorium, erecting indoor staging to reach the domed ceiling five stories overhead. Like Michelangelo pressed against the Sistine Chapel ceiling, inch by inch, workers uncovered the painted patterns from the original Peirce family decor.

"This is the largest and most flamboyant decorative element I've ever had the pleasure of uncovering," said architectural conservator Bryon Roesselet of EverGreene Architectural Arts, Inc. Roesselet had previously completed projects at the U.S. Capitol, the Lincoln Memorial, and the New York Public Library.

Workers revealed painted neo-classic decorations, scrolls, and patterned designs. Adding fresh paint, rich colors, and subtle lighting telegraphed a century-old message to Music Hall visitors in their seats far below. The show begins, ladies and gentlemen, from the moment you enter this hallowed hall. In a city rich with history, but increasingly beset by generic new buildings, simply taking one's seat in New Hampshire's oldest surviving theater is a carriage ride into bygone days.

ABOVE: *Uncovering the decorative features of a bygone era was a costly, time-consuming, and thrilling process. Here an expert restorer brings back a figure almost lost to history. Photo by Quentin Stockwell. (MHC)*

The icing on the cake was a new chandelier created over eighteen months by the Lighting Center at Rockingham Electric. The elegant and stately fixture, five by five feet, has five tiers of long crystal strands. Custom-made and energy-efficient, the new fixture mirrors the ornate 1878 chandelier.

If the restored auditorium was a portal to the past, the next phase was a trip through the looking glass. From its creation the ground floor lobby of the Music Hall had been a cramped, often chilly, waystation. By the twenty-first century, despite upgrades, the lobby remained an uninspired entrance with cracked flooring, an outdated box office, and antique bathrooms that rated somewhere between funky and foreboding. To expand the drab lobby into a dramatic new public space, however, meant hammering through solid rock.

"Few people realized there was no basement under the auditorium," says John Merkle, lead architect on the decade-long

Music Hall project. "We had a small mining operation in there and we took out about 700 cubic yards of rock ledge from beneath the theater." The resulting excavation, completed while the Music Hall was still in operation, doubled the size of the lobby.

Whatever occupied that new lobby space, Music Hall planners understood, would come to define not only the theater but the city itself. The new $2.2 million "Founders Lobby," would echo the Beaux Arts style, the same lavish, heavily ornamental classical design that had inspired the early designers. The new lobby also had to be ecologically and economically "green," strikingly modern, and it had to highlight the history of the theater. "The challenge of it," Merkle says today, "was really one of the more difficult things that I have ever had to work on."

Installing electricity, HVAC, and plumbing into what amounted to an underground cave was occasionally "a nightmare," Merkle admits. But the scariest moment occurred in May as Barbara Walters, the "first lady of American journalism," was

wrapping up her lecture during a sold-out episode of "Writers on a New England Stage."

Suddenly the balcony audience felt the ground shudder beneath them. A brick support in the lobby construction area below had shifted approximately an eighth of an inch, causing no damage or injuries. The building was evacuated and Ms. Walters was whisked away in a limousine. "She really brought down the house," one bystander reported.

Delivered on budget and on deadline, the new lobby opened to public view on September 19, 2008, timed to the tenth anniversary of "Telluride by the Sea."

"Nobody told me they hated it," Merkle laughs, "but they certainly were shocked." The finished lobby, designed in part by Minneapolis artist Jason McLean, was "beyond spectacular." and "jaw-dropping" and "a real stunner," visitors exclaimed. Everyone saw something different. Guests imagined themselves transported to an enchanted forest or an alien spaceship, to a medieval European village, or submerged beneath the sea in a whimsical Jules Verne-style submarine. Journalists struggled to attach words to the mind-bending landscape with its sculpted brass forest of trees, vines, and leaves dotted with glowing transparent plastic cubes and held together by pearlescent Corinthian pillars, tumbledown stone walls, and tiled walkways.

Who could have predicted that one of New Hampshire's "must-see" attractions has become the surreal men's and women's lobby lavatories? Meanwhile, the history of the Music Hall is told in the custom-made lobby wallpaper that incorporates archival items such as old playbills, ticket stubs, and photographs. In addition to a friendly windowless new box office and a quirky concession stand and service bar, the curved central space is dotted with velvet Victorian settees and wired with colorful LED lights that can be altered to suit any mood.

"We imagined a young girl or boy from a neighboring town coming to Portsmouth in the late 1800s being knocked out by the beauty and grandeur of the Music Hall," Patricia Lynch says. "I didn't want a bank lobby. I wanted a magical place."

ABOVE: *The custom-made, energy-efficient new chandelier replaced the former Civic lighting feature — a series of light bulbs attached to a trash can lid — that had served since the original chandelier was sold off decades ago. (DJM)*

OPPOSITE: *Unlike anything Portsmouth had ever seen, the creation of the Founders Lobby required removing 700 cubic feet of rock from beneath the historic theater, pouring a new floor, and designing decorative elements for an unforgettable Beaux Arts-style gathering place with a unique bar, restrooms, and ticket booth. (MHC)*

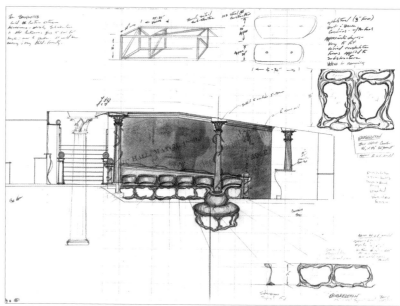

ABOVE: *View of the completed lower lobby with its whimsical Beaux Arts design. (MHC)*

RIGHT: *Sketch of design details for the proposed Founders Lobby. (MHC)*

Vision quest

"Patricia Lynch has led what has been a vast transformation of a facility that had been in disrepair for years," the *NH Business Review* affirmed after the lobby premiere. That change had come, Lynch told the *Review,* "because people were willing to think bigger than they had before. There are so many people who have contributed to this."

"Vision is not about saying one will do great things," Lynch says today. "That is not vision. That is simply an exercise in self-promotion. Vision is actually grounded in reality. It's about surveying the territory to see forward to a horizon that is within one's grasp. I always take time to do my homework."

Developing diverse audiences, Lynch knew, created diverse revenue streams. Each signature series like "Telluride by the Sea" and "Writers on a New England Stage," drew its own unique crowd. The music series "Intimately Yours" featured well-known artists like Graham Nash, Suzanne Vega, Aaron Neville, Emmylou Harris, Ziggy Marley, and Wynton Marsalis. For opera buffs the Metropolitan Opera broadcasts come directly from Lincoln Center in New York. "Hilarity" delivers top comics including Steve Martin, Jay Leno, and Paula Poundstone. There are series for kids, for cinephiles, for theater and symphony lovers.

ABOVE: *New Hampshire documentary film-maker Ken Burns joins another Music Hall supporter Maxine Morse during a special event at the Loft. (DJM)*

ABOVE: *Comedians Whoopi Goldberg (top) and Jay Leno (bottom) take center stage at the historic Music Hall where Mark Twain once stood. (DJM)*

Her formula for success is to stay consistent, stay excellent, and keep your eye on the latest trends.

"The worst thing you can do with an audience is promise them good things and then give them mediocre," Lynch says. "I don't get involved in discussions of high or low culture. To me it's all show business, and the very nature of show business is that you rely on one another to deliver the best."

As to management style, the executive director imagines the Music Hall as a hub surrounded by "circles of visionary leaders." There are leaders among her circle of trustees, among the circle of donors, among the theater staff, and among volunteers. These leaders bring their special skills to keep the circles spinning.

"I think I'm funny," Lynch says, when pressed to describe her personal style. "I know I'm irreverent. But it's true I do not suffer fools gladly, that's for damn sure, and everybody knows that. They also know I'm a nut about quality."

"I always refer to Patty as a high-speed locomotive," says "ex officio" trustee Jameson French. "She has a remarkable abundance of energy and creative thinking that has energized a lot of what's going on. She sometimes drives me crazy, but you've got to love her for it. She is a person of substantial influence."

"What's wonderful about all of this," Lynch says today, "is that together all of us have grown. People have learned to take more risks because of me, and I have learned to be more generous because of them."

Creating a family

Looking back, it's still hard to believe the Music Hall renovation with its magical Beaux Arts lobby happened without a touch of sorcery. It all came together amid dismal financial times. During the few years since the Friends had saved their landmark theater from the wrecking ball, housing values along the seacoast had doubled. But in 2004, the year Patricia Lynch arrived, the bubble burst. Declining real estate values led to a $700 billion federal bank bailout and the "Great Recession" of 2008.

The Friends pressed on, determined to be one of the top performing arts centers in New England and a key driver of the local economy. The diversified "branded" programming plan was working. Membership was up. Tickets sales were strong. Business owners were discovering that a big night at the Music Hall also meant a big night for downtown bars, shops, and restaurants. But behind the scenes, hitting the $13.5 million mark of the capital campaign was still a daunting target. The original founders had already dug deep and many were experiencing "donor fatigue."

At one point Gail VanHoy Carolan, then co-chair of the capital campaign, reached out to a fellow fundraiser, who was also a key benefactor. "It was in that recessionary time," Carolan now says. "I can remember being in my dining room and calling her up and saying — My God, I'm stuck. I can't move the needle. And she said — Put a million dollars down from me for a legacy gift. And it kick-started us again and got us going. There were a lot of heroes in that campaign."

Heroes continued to arrive. As the economy slowly revived, new people and new businesses joined an ever-widening circle of donors. Half a dozen founding "stakeholders" have grown to over sixty at this writing.

"That's the life of the theater," Music Hall CFO Tina Sawtelle says today. "The show never stops and neither does the fundraising. This beautiful old theater will always need work. Booking live shows is costly. Competition is fierce. Technology keeps evolving."

To survive, thrive, and grow, Sawtelle says, the theater relies on constant fundraising for almost a third of its revenue. The impact creates an upward spiral. Rather than focusing entirely on

ABOVE: *(top) Deputy Director of Programming Therese LaGamma (center) backstage with singer-songwriters Shawn Colvin and Emmylou Harris. (MHC)*

ABOVE: *(bottom) Legendary performer Tony Bennett backstage at the Music Hall. (DJM)*

ABOVE: *Another success as the Music Hall challenges the community to "Fill the Hall" with bags of food to be donated to a worthy charity. (DJM)*

RIGHT: *Opera megastar Renee Fleming (center) pictured with longtime key supporters and visionary leaders (left to right) Gail Carolan, Kathleen Murray, Chris Dwyer, and Michael Huxtable.(DJM)*

survival, as in its early days, the flow of donor funds has allowed the Music Hall to offer more aggressive programming and to take creative risks as with its collaborations with the Ogunquit Playhouse. The result, so far, has been a series of Broadway-style musicals, including Disney's *Beauty and the Beast,* Irving Berlin's *White Christmas, Elf the Musical,* and *Annie.* Each holiday production featured a live orchestra, professional actor-singer-dancers, and original set design, scenery, and effects. The multi-week holiday shows have become the highest revenue-generating events in Music Hall history, delighting audiences of all ages. Superior programming, says Gail VanHoy Carolan, drives ticket sales to a wider, more diversified audience. And ticket sales motivate more sponsors in a rising spiral of success.

"The point I really want to make," Carolan says, "is that this is a very unique community of people. I think they truly get it. They have a lot of pride of ownership in this theater, and they understand that they are investing money in the future."

"I think we've got a lot of wind in our sails now," she adds. "If you get this right — someone said to me once — you're going to transform this town."

LEFT: Holiday musical productions like Irving Berlin's White Christmas *performed by the Ogunquit Playhouse have become the most anticipated and successful events of the year at the Music Hall. Pictured are Kate Loprest, Joey Sorge, Jeffry Denman, Vanessa Sonon, and the 2015 cast. (DJM)*

Future tense

But back in the year 2008, as the Founders Lobby opened up and the Great Recession dragged on, no one knew if the next phase of the Music Hall renovation plan was even possible.

"What's left to do? There is so much," board president Mike Harvell announced during the theater's Vintage Christmas festivities on the brink of 2009. "However, it's still touch and go as to whether we'll get it all done."

The theater's critical infrastructure was worn out, Harvell said. The backstage was still operating with nineteenth-century technology. There was no room in the building for expanding community and educational programs or for added office staff. Worse yet, in the risky world of live and costly performances, the Music Hall had no "rainy day funds" and no significant endowment. And so, Harvell concluded, "While it seems we have arrived — we are only just gathering our breath as we set off again."

One tiny step forward fizzled. In 2009 the theater asked permission to change the name of its portion of Chestnut Street to Music Hall Way. Once three blocks long, Chestnut had run from Congress Street, the city's main artery, to Court Street, now the site of the African Burying Ground Memorial. But in the 1970s a new parking lot had cut Chestnut into two disconnected segments, each retaining the same name. The confusion to visitors in search of the Music Hall was obvious.

"If we go nitpicking and changing," one longtime resident argued, "we'll have nothing left of the original city." But city councilor Chris Dwyer argued in response that the names of almost all downtown streets had been changed at least once to suit the times. Chestnut had been Prison Lane when there was a prison and then changed to Elm Street in 1828 when there were elms. The city council, however, turned down the request by a vote of six to two.

The next big hurdle was to locate office space. There had never been enough administrative room in the theater. In the early twentieth century F.W. Hartford, and later his son Justin, had worked from their newspaper office at the foot of Chestnut Street. For years the Friends had been running the show out of a crowded suite of rented rooms in the old brick Kearsarge

ABOVE: *Board president Jay McSharry celebrates the newly completed streetscape and arch in 2018. (DJM)*

OPPOSITE: *(top) A hard hat tour of the new Loft theater space during final construction. The newer, smaller, high-tech Loft stage allows for hundreds of annual meetings, lectures, films, author events, and concerts, including affordable shows by an incredible variety of local performers. (DJM)*

OPPOSITE: *(bottom) The addition of a second facility just a block from the historic Music Hall was another game changer. The Loft on Congress Street includes a ticketing facility, bar, stage, and upstairs offices. (KAR)*

building next door at 104 Congress. Built as a two-family dwelling just after the Civil War by the same Peirce family who owned the Music Hall, the Kearsarge House (named for a famous Portsmouth battleship) was later converted into a grand downtown hotel. Known for its bow-fronted exterior and an impressive mahogany and chestnut central staircase, the restored Kearsarge has since leased space to shops, a restaurant, a delicatessen, and a lounge.

After long and careful planning the Music Hall launched its boldest venture to date. The Friends purchased a two-story building, once a bridal and formal wear shop, across from the Kearsarge at 131 Congress Street. "The Loft" opened in 2011 and instantly solved myriad vexing issues.

At first glance the Loft looks like a chic full-service bar visible to the city's main street through floor-to-ceiling windows. A busy ticketing station is situated just inside the glass doors at street level. Oversized photos of famous Music Hall performers are mounted on hurricane fencing and acoustic panels against bare concrete walls. Unlike its sweeping curvaceous Victorian sibling, the Loft is angular and industrial, yet intimate.

Upstairs provides sunny modern offices for a growing professional staff. The downstairs is a compact, flexible theater. The alternate theater is ideal for lectures, concerts, discussion or school groups, community events, workshops, art films, and meetings. When 900 seats in the historic hall are too many, the 124-seat Loft is the obvious solution.

With movable seating, cabaret tables, a thirty-two-foot stage, a fifteen-foot movie screen, and state-of-the-art digital equipment, the Loft stage is as adaptable as a Swiss Army knife. "Live at the Loft," for instance, features emerging, local, and diverse musicians in a nightclub setting. "Writers at the Loft," meanwhile, offers booklovers a chance to meet their favorite authors in a more cozy environment, to ask questions, and to move up from popcorn to cocktails.

"The Loft is all about discovery," says music curator and producer Thérèse LaGamma, who spends her days and nights "out in the field" searching the eastern seaboard for the next great act. To date, hundreds of artists from vintage country singers and punk rockers to breakout bands from Mexico and Ukraine have

ABOVE: *The exterior of the Loft on Congress Street in downtown Portsmouth, New Hampshire. (DJM)*

played the Loft stage. The smaller format is also ideal for showcasing talented locals. Many of the emerging musicians move on to headline festivals and much larger rooms or return to play the historic Music Hall. "Artists love the intimacy of the room," LaGamma says, "and we love introducing our discoveries to Portsmouth patrons."

Back out on the street, the city is booming. The cultural revival that began with Theatre by the Sea half a century before is now in evidence on every block. New eateries, coffee bars, boutiques, pubs, and art galleries seem to materialize overnight. Within view of the Loft, two conjoined, 1810-era brick buildings have become Discover Portsmouth, a nonprofit welcome center with a focus on local history and culture. As hotels spring up in the nearby North End, once decimated by urban renewal, the nonprofit 3S Artspace carries on its mission to support bold emerging arts and entertainment. Further down Islington Street, the city's West End has become an alternate hotspot.

Two hundred years after the economy crashed and the city burned, New Hampshire's only seaport is back in the limelight. These days travel websites frequently list Portsmouth among the nation's most historic, most attractive, most walkable destinations. One travel writer called Portsmouth "quite possibly the most magical city in America." Another claims Portsmouth is the fifth best small city on the planet. Locals take it all, as Yankees must, with more than a grain of sea salt.

At the center of all this, miraculously, the Music Hall still stands, as old as HMS *Pinafore* and as young as the latest garage band. Imagining all the talented people who have spoken, acted, danced, and made music on these same few square feet of staging bends the mind. Imagining Portsmouth without them breaks the heart.

Amid the 2017 holiday season the Music Hall replaced its aging plywood sign with a brilliantly colored, energy-efficient, digital marquee. A dazzling illuminated neon "blade" now rises from the marquee to the rooftop, highlighting the theater like never before. Designed by the Music Hall team, manufactured in Ohio, the sign is so much more than a network of gas-filled blown-glass tubes powered by banks of humming transformers. It's a message, a beacon, and a trophy all in one.

ABOVE: *The entrance to one of the otherworldly "must-see" restrooms in the Music Hall lower lobby. (BDP)*

ABOVE: *The new neon "blade" Music Hall marquee brightens the new year in downtown Portsmouth. (DJM)*

"There's nothing off-the-shelf around here," laughs director of operations Michael Tucker. "Patricia loves a challenge and she wanted something iconic. Our goal, you could say, was to bring some of the inside outside."

Watching the sign light up, Tucker says, was an inspirational moment. "It opened everybody's eyes to the possibility of doing the unimaginable," he says. "Everybody feels empowered. As employees of the Music Hall, we're always saying we could build a better engine while we're flying the plane."

Two decades in the planning, the marquee is the glittering jewel in the crown of an $800,000 streetscape initiative between the Friends of the Music Hall and the City of Portsmouth. Six months later, in June of 2018, police diverted downtown traffic as workmen hoisted a massive thirty-seven-foot-tall metal arch into place at the base of Chestnut Street. Built of steel and aluminum and coated with bronze, the 10,000 pound sculpture, paid for by theater sponsors, completes the pedestrian-friendly design. One leg of the arch stands in front of the old Hartford family newspaper offices while the other highlights the Peirce family's stately Kearsarge House. It was a fitting memorial to the elegantly dressed theater on its 140th birthday.

It may not matter to out-of-towners, or even to most locals, but the symbolism of the giant arch is deeply rooted in Portsmouth history. Two centuries ago, when times were tough, the city threw a big party. The party became a tradition. Prodigal sons and daughters who had abandoned their hometown for greener pastures were invited back. Great arches made of wood and festooned with flags, greenery, and welcoming messages appeared all over the Old Town by the Sea.

Those great homecoming arches were designed to guide the crowds to the heart of Market Square. There were lots of speeches back in the day, plenty of music, and an abundance of food and drink. Our forebears liked to tell stories about the way things used to be in a rough and tumble seaport. They recalled, with no small sense of pride, that their ancestors were an independent bunch who preferred feasting to fasting. They raised glasses full of Frank Jones ale and toasted the ragged band of settlers who, having sailed down the mighty Piscataqua River, stepped tentatively off their wooden ship carrying one Bible, two drums, and fifteen oboes. ❧

ABOVE: *For centuries Portsmouth has welcomed visitors with ceremonial arches. The towering metal arch, plus the neon marquee and the redesigned pedestrian streetscape on Chestnut Street, mark the fulfillment of a fifteen-year vision to create a world-class performance center, the "beating heart" of the cultural renaissance on the New Hampshire seacoast. (DJM)*

Illustration & Photo Credit Abbreviations

AAS	American Antiquarian Society	MHS	Massachusetts Historical Society
ATH	Portsmouth Athenaeum Collection	MIS	Miscellaneous sources
BDF	Blind Dog Photo	NAG	The National Art Gallery
BMC	British Museum Collection	NLS	The National Library of Scotland
CDM	Charles Dickens Museum	NHH	New Hampshire Historical Society
DJM	David J. Murray, ClearEyePhoto.com	NHT	NH Theatre Project
DRI	Drika Overton	NYP	New York Public Library
GBP	George Barker Photography	OPH	Ogunquit Playhouse
GCC	Garrick Club Collection	PAA	Bill Paarlberg
GEN	Generic Theatre	PHS	Portsmouth Historical Society
GUN	Gundalow Company	PON	Pontine Movement Theatre
HAL	James Haller	PPL	Portsmouth Public Library
HMA	Hood Museum of Art, Dartmouth College	RAN	Random House
HTC	Harvard Theatre Collection	SBM	Strawbery Banke Museum Collection
JDR	J. Dennis Robinson (author's collection)	SHS	Sandwich Historical Society
JSP	Joe Stevens Photography	TJW	T.J. Wheeler
KAR	Rob Karosis Photography	TPR	The Press Room
KLC	Kevin LaFond Collection	USM	U.S. Marine Corp
LIZ	Liz Lerman	WBF	Walter Brooks Family
LOC	Library of Congress	WHH	White House Historical Association
MET	The Met	WIK	Wikipedia, Wikimedia Commons
MHC	Music Hall Collection	WIN	Scott Weintraub

OPPOSITE: *Russian National Ballet Theatre performing Swan Lake (DJM)*

Selected Bibliography

Altschiller, Howard. "An evening with an author." *Portsmouth Herald*, October 29, 2010.

Anonymous. "Frank Jones is dying." *New York Times,* January 19, 1902.

Anonymous. "The theatre that couldn't happen," (Theatre by the Sea). *The Beacon*, January 1976.

Auerbach, Nina. "Dickens and Acting Women." In *Dramatic Dickens,* edited by MacKay, C.H. London: Palgrave Macmillan, 1989.

Augusta, Phil. "The decline and fall of Theatre by the Sea." *Re: Ports*, April 10, 1987.

Baenen, Michael. "The Portsmouth Athenaeum Reading Room: the biography of a space." *Piscataqua Decorative Arts Society, Volume I, 2002-2003 Lecture Series.* Portsmouth, NH: Peter E. Randall Publisher, 2004.

Bailey, Susan. "Problems, but none of them insurmountable." *Portsmouth Herald*, February 9, 1986.

Barry, Dan. "Left at the theater long ago, and bringing the place to life." *New York Times,* July 21, 2008.

Benes, Peter. *For a Short Time Only: Itinerants and the Resurgence of Popular Culture in Early America.* Amherst: University of Massachusetts Press, 2016.

Bode, Carl. *The American Lyceum: Town Meeting of the Mind.* Carbondale: Southern Illinois University Press, 1968.

Bodnar, Steven and Jeanne McCartin. "Music Hall wows 'em." *Portsmouth Herald*, September 20, 2008.

Brewster, Charles W. *Rambles about Portsmouth.* Portsmouth, NH: L.W. Brewster, 1873.

Brewster, Lewis (editor). *Portsmouth Journal.* Portsmouth Athenaeum archives, 1877.

Brighton, Raymond. *Frank Jones: King of the Alemakers.* Portsmouth, NH: Peter E. Randall Publisher, 1985.

——. *Rambles about Portsmouth.* Portsmouth, NH: Peter E. Randall Publisher, 1994.

——. *They Came to Fish.* Portsmouth, NH: Peter E. Randall Publisher, 1979.

Brooks, Walter. An unpublished taped interview with former Civic Theatre manager. Friends of the Music Hall, 1980s.

Burroughs, Charles. *An Address of Female Education.* Portsmouth, NH: Childs & March, 1827. (Google Books)

Candee, Richard M. "Thomas P. Moses: artist, musician & poet of Portsmouth, New Hampshire." *Antiques & Fine Art Magazine,* 2002.

——. (editor). *Building Portsmouth: The Neighborhoods & Architecture of New Hampshire's Oldest City.* Portsmouth, NH: Portsmouth Advocates, Inc, Back Channel Press, 2006.

——. Notes related to Thomas P. Moses conversion and decoration of the Cameneum. (Research files)

Carroll, Carole Lee, Bunny Hart, and Susan Day Meffert. *The Ogunquit Playhouse: 75 Years, America's Foremost Summer Theatre.* Portsmouth, NH: Back Channel Press, 2007.

Clark, Martha Fuller. Friends of the Music Hall archival records 1980s. Music Hall Collection.

Clark, Orange. *A Discourse on Family Discipline.* San Francisco, 1860. (pamphlet on Google Books).

Cockrell, Dale. *Demons of Disorder: Early Blackface Minstrels and their World.* Cambridge University Press, 1997.

Crawford, Robert W. *In Art We Trust: the Board of Trustees in the Performing Arts.* New York: Drama Pub, 1982.

Cullen, Frank, Florence Hackman, and Donald McNeilly. *Vaudeville, Old & New: an Encyclopedia of Variety Performers in America.* New York: Routledge, 2007.

Cummins, Sharon. "Hartwig was the force behind little theatre," Seacoastonline.com, September 18, 2008.

Davies, Rev. Thomas F. *Memoir of Joshua Winslow Peirce.* Boston: For Private Distribution, 1874.

Davis, William A. "Portsmouth: it seems so far away." *Boston Sunday Globe,* January 9, 1977.

Dobson, Michael, and Nigel Cliff. "The Shakespeare Riots: Revenge, Drama and Death in 19th-Century America." *The London Review of Books.* 29: 15, 2007.

Downs, Winfield Scott. "Hon. Fernando W. Hartford." *Encyclopedia of American Biography.* New York: The American Historical Company, New Series, Volume 11, pp. 273-5, 1940.

Elliott, Chris. "The Music Hall celebrates milestone with 1878 reprise." *Portsmouth Herald,* October 7, 2003.

Ferriter, Tom (editor). "Renaissance city on the seacoast." Special edition, *New Hampshire Times,* November 4, 1981.

Flynn, George. "Portsmouth Combination." *The Moving Picture World,* May 25, 1916.

"Franklin Block Report." *The National Register of Historic Places Inventory Registration* form U.S. Department of the Interior, National Park Service, 1984.

Freeman, Jr., Castle. "Benning Wentworth: brief life of a colonial grandee 1696-1770." *Harvard Magazine,* November-December, 2004.

French, Jameson. Author interview and correspondence.

Garvin, James. "First balloon over New Hampshire." SeacoastNH.com.

Gillette, Christine. "Gabel leaving Music Hall." *Portsmouth Herald,* July 2, 2003.

Gillis, Michael. "Poetry in motion pictures." *Showcase Magazine/Foster's Daily Democrat,* September 18, 2003.

Gooding, Alfred (editor). *The Portsmouth Book.* Boston: George Ellis, 1899.

Goot, Dan. "Author (Dan Brown) takes Portsmouth stage." *Foster's Daily Democrat,* April 24, 2006.

Grady, John. "Theaters aid Portsmouth business." *NH Business Review,* November 3, 1989.

——. "Time for a new team of dreamers." *NH Seacoast Sunday,* September 21, 1986.

Hackett, Frank W. *Memoir of Hom. William H. Y. Hackett.* Boston: Rand, Avery & Company, 1879. (Google Books)

Hackett, Hon. William H. Y. "Opening night address of Portsmouth Music Hall." *Portsmouth Daily Chronicle,* January 30, 1878.

Halliburton, Andrew. *Essays of Andrew Halliburton.* Portsmouth: Charles Brewster, 1847.

Harvell, Michael. "Music Hall's progress great, but long way to go." *Portsmouth Herald* (letter to the editors), November 28, 2008.

Hawthorne, Nathaniel. *The Blithedale Romance.* Penguin Books, 1983 (originally 1852).

Hench, David. "Portsmouth Music Hall owner says he's losing money, wants help." *Foster's Daily Democrat,* April 20, 1988.

Hertz, Sue. "Time and tide in Portsmouth," *The Boston Globe Magazine,* April 24, 1982.

Hodgdon, John A. *Richard Potter: America's First Black Celebrity.* Charlottesville: University of Virginia Press, 2017.

Holbrook, Josiah. *The American Lyceum, or Society for the Improvement of Schools and Diffusion of Useful Knowledge.* Boston, 1829.

Holly, Bill, and Herbert D. Waldron. *Love Letters to Spike: a Telegrapher's Lament, with a Brief, Eclectic History of Communications in the Seacoast.* Portsmouth, NH: Placenames Press, 2004.

Hopper, Jeff. "Social dancing at the Assembly House." Silkdamask.org, February 24, 2107.

Ingmire, Bruce. "Griffin family with a gravedigger." *Portsmouth Press,* February 3, 1991.

——. "Peirce family fortune declined in 20th century," *Portsmouth Press,* November 14, 1991.

John, Farmer (Farmer's Almanac). *The New Hampshire Register and United States Calendar for 1827.* Concord, NH: Jacob B. Moore, 1826.

Josselyn, John. *An Account of Two Voyages to New-England, Made during the Years 1638, 1663.* Boston: William Veazie, 1865. (Google Books)

Kahan, Gerald, and George Alexander Stevens. *George Alexander Stevens and the Lecture on Heads.* Athens: University of Georgia Press, 1984.

Kane, Debbie. "A new performance space in Portsmouth." *New Hampshire Home,* November-December, 2011.

Kelly, Margaret Whyte. *Sarah: Her Story: the Life Story of Sarah Parker Rice Goodwin, Wife of Ichabod Goodwin, New Hampshire's Civil War Governor.* Portsmouth, NH: Back Channel Press, 2006.

Kences, James. "Village harmony: music and popular culture in Portsmouth, New Hampshire." *Dublin Seminar for New England Folklore.* Boston: Boston University, 1998.

Khrapak, Vyacheslav. "Reflections on the American Lyceum: the legacy of Josiah Holbrook and the transcendental sessions." *Journal of Philosophy & History of Education,* University of Oklahoma Vol. 64, No. 1, pp. 47–62, 2014.

Killeen, Wendy. "Three cultural organizations looking for new directors." *Boston Globe,* September 25, 2003.

Kilton, George W. "Temperance in Portsmouth." May 31, 1840 letter, reprinted in *Christian Journal,* June 6, 1844.

Kittredge, Clare. "Now playing in Portsmouth," *Boston Sunday Globe,* June 7, 1987.

Knowlton, H.L. "Col. John H. Bartlett." Concord, NH: *The Granite Monthly,* Vol. 8, No. 6, pp. 135-138, May, 1913.

Laffoley, Steven Edwin. *Shadowboxing: the Rise and Fall of George Dixon.* Lawrencetown Beach: Pottersfield Press, 2012.

Lawlor, Richard. "Civic Theater to live again." *Rockingham Gazette,* July 24, 1985.

Lee, Eliza Buckminster. *Memoirs of Rev. J. Buckminster ... and of his Son Rev. J.S. Buckminster.* Boston: Crosby and Nichols, 1849.

Leech, Adam. "Music Hall request to rename street is denied." *Portsmouth Herald,* October 2009.

Lehman, Eric D. *Becoming Tom Thumb: Charles Stratton, P.T. Barnum, and the Dawn of American Celebrity.* Middletown, CT: Wesleyan University Press, 2013.

Lerman, Liz. *Hiking the Horizontal: Field Notes from a Choreographer.* Middletown CT: Wesleyan University Press, 2014.

Library of Congress. Edison Collection: Shift to Projectors and the Vitascope (1895-1896). loc.gov.

LoMonaco, Martha Schmoyer. "Actor, Audience, and Art: Theatre in Portsmouth, New Hampshire, 1791-1801." (thesis) Tufts University, 1981.

Long, Tom. "Theater enters a new stage." *Boston Sunday Globe,* July 16, 2006.

Lord, Lewis J. "Old New England port rescues its vanishing charm." (undated article)

MacKay, Carol Hanbery. *Dramatic Dickens.* Basingstoke, UK: Macmillan Press, 1989.

Mandell, Jeffrey. "Focus on survival: Hampton Cinemas" (interview with Walter Brooks), *Business NH,* July 1984.

Marzloff, Karen. "Master of arts: Patricia Lynch writes the next chapter of the Music Hall." *The Wire,* April 7, 2004.

Maxine, David. "A Production History of the 1903 Oz." Theatre Division, New York Public Library for the Performing Arts, (Hungry Tiger Press). December 15, 2011, www.nypl.org.

McCartin, Jeanne. "'Neighborhoods' leads us into the 21st century." *Spotlight Magazine,* January 18, 2001.

McMenemy, Jeff. "Using arts to grow the local economy." *Portsmouth Herald,* September 30, 2016.

Merkle, John, TMS Architects, and Preservation Company. "Historic Structures Report Music Hall, Portsmouth, New Hampshire." *NH Division of Historic Resources,* 2005.

Newspaper articles from *Portsmouth Herald, Portsmouth Chronicle, Portsmouth Times, Portsmouth Journal of Literature and Politics, Manchester Union Leader, York Weekly, Portsmouth Magazine, Women for Women Weekly, Seacoast Sunday, Foster's Daily Democrat* and other local newspapers.

Morris, Zhana, and Trevor F. Bartlett. *The Music Hall, Portsmouth.* Charleston, SC: Arcadia Press, 2003.

Morris, Zhana (Music Hall historian) "Database of Music Hall Performances," other research files, Music Hall Archives, and blogs on themusichall.org.

Music Hall archives including posters, programs, and newspaper clippings archived at the Portsmouth Athenaeum.

NHBR editors. "Q&A with the Music Hall's Patricia Lynch." *NH Business Review,* January 30, 2009.

NH Historical Society, *Collections of the New Hampshire Historical Society,* Volume 2.. Boston: Jacob B. Moore, 1827.

Palmer, Greg (writer) and Fenster, Rosemary Garner. *Vaudeville.* New York, NY: KCTS Television, American Masters Special, 1999.

Peirce, Frederick Clifton. *Peirce Genealogy, Being the Record of the Posterity of John Pers...with Notes on the History of Other Families of Peirce, Pierce, Pearce, etc.* C. Hamilton: Worcester, MA, 1880. (Google books)

Philbrick, Rodman. "Switch on the footlights." *New Hampshire Profiles,* February 1986.

Philpot, Chelsey. "Portsmouth, NH established itself as a cultural hub." *Boston Globe,* July 6, 2014.

Pichierri, Louis. *Music in New Hampshire 1623-1800.* New York: Columbia University Press, 1960.

Pierce, Robert, Drika Overton, Bill Eidson, Paul Arslanian, and Ken Lacouture. *Four Theatres: Remembering Portsmouth in the Age of Vaudeville.* Portsmouth, NH. (DVD) 2004.

Pope, Laura (editor/author). 2017. *Becoming Portsmouth: Voices from a Half Century of Change.* Charleston, SC: The History Press, 2017.

——. "The nonprofit challenge: executive directors leave three key Portsmouth venues." *Portsmouth Times,* October 5, 2003.

Portsmouth Athenaeum Special Collections including Hartford Family records, Allied Theatres Company Account Books (1916-1919), Portsmouth Theatre Company (1903-1945), Portsmouth Music Hall, Portsmouth Lyceum Meeting Records (1834-1853), and Theatre by the Sea archives (1968-1987).

——. Vertical file for The Shipyard Project, Music, Theater, Portsmouth Lyceum, and others.

Portsmouth City Directories, 1877-1882

Portsmouth Lyceum. *Portsmouth Lyceum. Prospectus.* Portsmouth, NH, January 1828 (New Hampshire Historical Society Archive, Concord, NH.)

Powell, E.P. "The rise and decline of the New England Lyceum." *The New England Magazine.* Vol. 17, No. 6 pp. 730–739, February 1895.

Rais, Paula (coordinator). *Telling Our Stories: Community Arts in Portsmouth 1992-2004,* Allegra Print and Imaging, NH Council on the Arts, 2004.

Randall, Peter E. *There are No Victors Here: A Local Perspective on the Treaty of Portsmouth.* Portsmouth, NH: Portsmouth Marine Society, 1985.

Richard, Ian. "Portsmouth Music Hall: culture gets a reprieve." *Sweet Potato,* February 26, 1986.

Richardson, Robert D. *Emerson: the Mind on Fire: a Biography.* Berkeley: University of California Press, 1997.

Roberts, Paige W. "The floral architect: notes and designs for processions." *Dublin Seminar for New England.* Boston University, 2000.

Robinson, J. Dennis. "The day Mark Twain wore black." SeacoastNH.com, *Portsmouth Herald, NH Gazette, Foster's Daily Democrat.*

——. "The Music Hall's gala return." *Rockingham Gazette,* October 30, 1985.

——. "First religious newspaper born in NH" (Elias Smith). *Portsmouth Herald,* March 28, 2011.

——. "Is it the last picture show in Portsmouth?" *Rockingham Gazette,* December 8, 1982.

——. "Who supports Portsmouth arts?" *Rockingham Gazette,* June 1, 1983.

——. "Prescott Park Arts Festival: people trying to put it together." *Rockingham Gazette,* April 13, 1983.

——. *Wentworth by the Sea: The Life and Times of a Grand Hotel.* Portsmouth, NH: Peter E. Randall Publisher, 2004.

——. *Strawbery Banke: A Seaport Museum 400 Years in the Making.* Portsmouth, NH: Published for Strawbery Banke Museum by Peter E. Randall Publisher, 2007.

——. "Portsmouth Herald seeks its own birthday." SeacoastNH.com

——. "Shifting street names is Portsmouth tradition." *Portsmouth Herald.* October 26, 2009.

——. "The deadly summer of 1912." SeacoastNH.com.

——. "Walter Brooks: he ran Portsmouth's movie theaters." *Rockingham Gazette.* December 8, 1982.

——. "Big risks at the Music Hall." *Rockingham Gazette,* July 26, 1985

——. "Remembering Aunt Rozzie Thaxter." *Portsmouth Herald,* January 9, 2017.

——. "The resurrection of Thomas P. Moses." SeacoastNH.com

——. "Frederick Douglass comes to town," *Portsmouth Herald*, August 11, 2011.

Rogers, Mary Cochrane. *Glimpses of an Old Social Capital (Portsmouth, New Hampshire) as Illustrated by the Life of the Reverend Arthur Browne and his Circle.* Boston: Printed for the subscribers, 1923.

Sagala, Sandra K. *Buffalo Bill on Stage.* Albuquerque: University of New Mexico Press, 2008.

Sammons, Mark, and Valerie Cunningham. *Black Portsmouth: Three Centuries of African-American Heritage.* Hanover, NH: University Press of New England, 2004.

Savage, Jack. "Revival is in the air." *NH Seacoast Sunday,* October 1, 1989.

Savin, Maynard. *Thomas William Robertson: His Plays and Stagecraft.* Providence: Brown University Studies, Vol 13, 1950.

Schell, Laura. "Larger than life: discovery and restoration of an 1878 'Buffalo Bill' billboard." *The Book & Paper Group Annual,* 2008.

Schultz, Steven. "Brubeck thrills crowd." *Foster's Daily Democrat,* October 4, 1989.

Sherman, George. *History of Temple Israel.* Portsmouth, NH: Self-published, 1997.

Smith, Elias. *The Life, Conversion, Preaching, Travels, and Sufferings of Elias Smith.* Portsmouth, NH: Printed by Beck & Foster, 1818.

Stackpole, Everett S. *The History of New Hampshire.* New York: The American Historical Society, 1916.

Stevens, George Alexander. *A Lecture on Heads ... with Additions by Mr. Pilon; as Delivered by Mr. Charles Lee Lewes. To which is added an Essay on Satire, etc. with Illustrations.* London: Vernor & Hood, 1802.

Strausbaugh, John. *Black Like You: Blackface, Whiteface, Insult & Imitation in American Popular Culture.* New York: Jeremy P. Tarcher, 2014.

Suffern, Richard Winslow, and Charles E. Clark. *From Graces to Gargoyles: a Social Essay on the Theater in Portsmouth, New Hampshire, 1762-1850.* Portsmouth: *Seacoast Arts Council,* 1972.

Tabor, John. "F.W. Hartford Founded Portsmouth Herald." *Literary Lions,* (J. Dennis Robinson, editor), NH Gazette and Portsmouth Athenaeum, 2006.

Temple, Robert. *The History of Harness Racing in New England* (on Elias M. Loew). Xlibris, 2010.

Tompkins, Eugene. *The History of the Boston Theatre, 1854-1901, compiled with the assistance of Quincy Kilby.* Boston: Houghton, Mifflin, 1908.

U.S. Navy, *Annual Report of the Navy Department,* 1900.

Untitled. (Portsmouth, NH) *U.S. News & World Report.* December 19, 1982.

Voas, Sharon. "A grand reopening in Portsmouth." *Concord Monitor,* February 26, 1986.

Warner, Jeffrey. Interview with noted musicologist and traditional music performer. www.jeffwarner.com

Watterson, Rodney K. *Whips to Walls: Naval Discipline from Flogging to Progressive-Era Reform at Portsmouth Prison.* Naval Institute Press, 2014.

Winslow, Richard Elliott. *"Do Your Job!": An Illustrated Bicentennial History of the Portsmouth Naval Shipyard, 1800-2000.* Portsmouth, NH: Portsmouth Marine Society, 2000.

Wood, Shari (editor). *Portsmouth Athenaeum: The Story of a Collection through the Eyes of Its Proprietors, 1817-2017.* Portsmouth, NH: Portsmouth Athenaeum, 2017.

Wright, Tom F. *The Cosmopolitan Lyceum Lecture Culture and the Globe in Nineteenth-Century America.* Amherst: University of Massachusetts Press, 2014.